GESTALT COUNSELLING
IN ACTION

SAGE COUNSELLING *IN ACTION*

Series Editor: WINDY DRYDEN

Sage Counselling in Action is a series of short, practical books developed especially for students and trainees. As accessible introductions to theory and practice, they have become core texts for many courses, both in counselling and other professions such as nursing, social work, teaching and management. Books in the series include:

Sue Culley and Tim Bond
Integrative Counselling Skills in Action, Second Edition

Windy Dryden and Michael Neenan
Rational Emotive Behavioural Counselling in Action, Third Edition

Michael Jacobs
Psychodynamic Counselling in Action, Third Edition

Diana Whitmore
Psychosynthesis Counselling in Action, Third Edition

Patricia D'Ardenne and Aruna Mahtani
Transcultural Counselling in Action, Second Edition

Ian Stewart
Transactional Counselling in Action, Second Edition

Dave Mearns and Brian Thorne
Person-Centred Counselling in Action, Second Edition

Petrūska Clarkson
Gestalt Counselling in Action, Third Edition

Tim Bond
Standards and Ethics for Counselling in Action, Second Edition

Peter Trower, Windy Dryden and Andrew Casey
Cognitive Behavioural Counselling in Action

GESTALT
COUNSELLING
IN ACTION
Third Edition

Petrūska Clarkson

 **SAGE** Publications
London • Thousand Oaks • New Delhi

First edition published 1989. Reprinted 1990, 1991, 1992,
1993 (twice), 1994, 1995, 1996, 1998, 2000
Second edition published 1999. Reprinted 2003
This third edition first published 2004

SAGE Publications Ltd
1 Oliver's Yard
55 City Road
London EC1Y 1SP

SAGE Publications Inc.
2455 Teller Road
Thousand Oaks, California 91320

SAGE Publications India Pvt Ltd
B-42, Panchsheel Enclave
Post Box 4109
New Delhi 110 017

British Library Cataloguing in Publication data

A catalogue record for this book is available from the British
Library

ISBN 1 4129 0084 0
ISBN 1 4129 0085 9 (pbk)

Library of Congress Control Number available

Typeset by M Rules
Printed in Great Britain by The Cromwell Press Ltd, Trowbridge, Wiltshire

*Empty is the argument of the philosopher who does not relive
any human suffering*

Epicurus

Contents

Preface

To write a book about psychotherapy is daunting. I painfully experience the chasm between the vividly alive encounter with another human being and the pale, static representation of the written word as it gropes towards some partial signification of our shared meanings in evolving dialogue.

I veer between the impossibility of doing justice to the fullness, the vibrancy, the immediacy of my client in his or her unique and idiosyncratic unfolding way of being and a desire to answer the questioning eyes of trainees and students wanting to 'read about it'. I thrill to the passionate, rich, full-blooded intelligence of Gestalt practice and chafe at the shackles imposed by the covers of a book.

I (and others) sometimes despair at the divergence and even contradictions between Gestalt theorists and sometimes delight in the creative freedom this bestows.

Gestalt is, above all, about the whole – smells, tastes, intuitions, the surrounding environment, the historical context, the planetary hologram. And all of these coexist like an excellent poem wherein which the artistry is never fully discovered, yet all the symbols and words, and cadences and shapes, interweave in a tapestry vibrating with life and tragedy and humour.

This is an introductory book in response to requests for an exposition of Gestalt accessible to beginning counsellors, following a temporal sequence and not dealing with more serious clinical disturbance. This editoral requirement dilutes from a therapeutic approach which values so highly the sudden coming-together moment of psychophysiological insight in perfect conjunction of right and left hemispheric functions in a single undivided moment. This book is but another beginning – a mere facet of what Gestalt can be – only one fragment of the living kaleidoscope, only a moment in eternity.

This is not a book about Gestalt, because the Gestalt that can be described is not Gestalt. It may indeed be a book *around* Gestalt. There is not one representation of a real client in this book, because any one of the real people I have worked with could never be captured in a book, still less in a few sentences. Their essence forever eludes description, their truth is veiled by my deliberate confusion of identities, life stories, words. Yet I hope that some of what they taught me shines through to light the way for others. The case study of Gary was contributed by Sue Fish, to whom I dedicate this book with appreciation and with love.

Preface to the Third Edition

I write this preface with deep appreciation for all the many people who have read and studied this book and found it valuable in the alleviation of human suffering and the development of human potential. I think that one of the major reasons for its continuing popularity and longevity is the fact that I wrote the original sticking close to the first sources, the first generation of Gestaltists and their immediate descendants. In this sense it is classical because first principles always remain the true foundation of any approach to psychotherapy.

In 1995, Rosenblatt contrasted 'the quintessential Fritz' with the 'quintessential conservative' approach to Gestalt, sharpening the polar contrasts between the Apollonian and the Dionysian spirits as follows:

Quintessential conservative	Quintessential Fritz
routinized, rational, bureaucratic	charismatic
scholarly, proper	rebellious
structured	anarchistic
organized	chaotic
civilized	primitive
asexual, spiritual	sexual
refined	vulgar
spectator, critic, audience	creative artist
serious	playful
bourgeois, Establishment	bohemian
cognitive	intuitive
professional	personal
soothing, placating	aggressive, destructive
intellectual	visceral, gutsy
dull, flat	lively

The Gestalt experiment, with its emphasis on ephemeral phenomenological awareness, and the injunction for both therapist and patient to take a risk and to take responsibility, offer an opportunity to Gestalt therapists to be creative *and* connected to the lively tradition of its founders (Rosenblatt, 1995: 47–48).

However, in the fourteen years since its first publication I have observed a tragic drift in many Gestalt organisations towards the 'quintessentially conservative' with the quintessentially Dionysian splitting off, dead, being exiled or operating independently outside a tightly regulated organisational and bureaucratic sphere ruled by a conventional conformity consensus. In my opinion, the true Dionysian Gestaltists, even after cleaning up their more ethically questionable antics, are now probably not always to be found listed on formal Gestalt Registers.

> Given the novelty and indefinite variety of the environment, no adjustment would be possible by the conservative inherited self-regulation alone; contact must be a *creative transformation* . . . On the other hand, creativity that is not continually destroying and assimilating an environment given in perception and resisting manipulation is useless to the organism and remains superficial and lacking in energy; it does not become deeply exciting, and it soon languishes. (Perls et al., 1951/1969: 406, italics added)

This creative transformation is individual realisation *and* collective co-evolution (Clarkson, 1991).

Our spiritual allegiance to Gestalt remains, because once having been beneficially infected by the genius of Gestalt, it is impossible to strip it from the blood and marrow of whatever we do – and however we live. So what is core?

At the heart of the Gestalt experience is Life's energy itself, the *élan vital* which has been identified with the pre-socratic term Physis. Perls wrote:

> Now normally the *élan vital*, the life force, energizes by sensing, by listening, by scouting, by describing the world – how is the world there. Now this life force apparently first mobilizes the center – *if* you have a center. And the center of the personality is what used to be called the soul: the emotions, the feelings, the spirit. (1969b: 63–64).

Physis or Phusis is an ancient Greek word very rich in meaning. It is used to refer to life energy as it manifests in nature, in growth and healing as well as in all dimensions of creativity. Physic/physician (as in medicine) and Physics (as in quantum/chaos understandings of the world) both derive from it. Here it is used as a concept to concentrate some of the most significant qualities and aspirations of Gestalt – in honour of everlasting change, unlearning as well as learning, living as well as dying well, the cycle as potent paradigm for human evolutionary processes, individual and culture, relationship and archetype, the importance of Nature as teacher and inspiration, the drive towards complexity, quality and wholeness, the co-existence of contradictions. Whether in individuals, couples, groups, organisations or artistic work, the central and organising theme is simply to have life – and to have it more abundantly.

I believe that we are all the servants of Physis, the life force or *élan vital* in psychotherapy – universal energy in its purest form (Clarkson, 1996b; 2002b). This is the soul of Gestalt which leads to a creative and aspirational ethic.

Perls, Hefferline and Goodman put it like this: 'Man does not strive to be good; the good is what it is human to strive for' (1951/1969: 335). In these words they are again articulating a philosophical position very similar to that of the Stoics who were grappling with this thousands of years ago in the following way:

> A good bootmaker is one who makes good boots, a good shepherd is one who keeps his sheep well, and even though good boots are in the Day-of-Judgement sense entirely worthless and fat sheep no whit better than starved sheep, yet the good bootmaker or good shepherd must do his work well or he will cease to be good.

> To be good he must perform his function . . . in performing that function there are certain things that he must 'prefer' to others, even though they are not really 'good'. He must prefer a healthy sheep or a well-made boot to their opposites . . . If a man is an artist, it is his function to produce beauty.
> (Murray, 1915: 126)

Or, if one is a bootmaker, to make good boots. On the Day of Judgement it hardly matters whether you made good boots, or whether you're chic, or fat or starving. But it matters that you were doing it well. It is this that Nature, or Physis, herself works when she shapes the seed into a tree or the blind puppy into a good hound. The perfection of the tree or the blind puppy is in itself indifferent, a thing of no ultimate value, 'Yet the goodness of Nature lies in working for that perfection' (Murray, 1915: 43). And our goodness lies in working for that perfection in serving humanity.

Thus the cycle or spiral of creative evolution continues from Heraclitus through the 'self' of Perls, Hefferline and Goodman, to the modern Gestalt of today.

The matter at issue in Heraclitus is physis . . . And correlative to the matter is a self-experience which is as deep as physis is comprehensive. The experience of physis is an experience of self for two reasons: (1) physis comprehends (encompasses) the self as it does everything else; and (2) the self is the locus where (for the human self) physis comprehends (understands) itself. Human experience is, in terms of physis, the self-experience of physis. (Guerrière, 1980: 129–30)

As I often say: 'Being yourself is the only thing you can ever be perfect at.' Or, in Fritz's words, 'May the force be with you.'

INTRODUCTION TO GESTALT

Definition of 'Gestalt'

The German word *Gestalt* is not easily translated into a single English term. It embraces such a wide variety of concepts: the shape, the pattern, the whole form, the configuration. It connotes the structural entity which is both different from and much more than the sum of its parts.

The idea of the family provides a useful example. A family is made up of separate members, each with his or her individual psychology. One could analyse each of them without seeing the others, but the way in which the family operates as a systemic whole is uniquely more than, and different from, the sum total of the individual psychologies of the family members.

The aim of the Gestalt approach is for a person to discover, explore and experience his or her own shape, pattern and wholeness. Analysis may be a part of the process, but the aim of Gestalt is the integration of all disparate parts. In this way people can let themselves become totally what they already are, *and* what they potentially can become. This fullness of experience can then be available to them both in the course of their life and in the experience of a single moment.

The Gestalt Approach to Counselling

The cognitive and experiential wholeness of every person, every moment, every event is similarly central to the Gestalt approach to counselling. There are some research indications that the two different hemispheres of the brain control different functions. These functions are not simplistically discrete but show a differential emphasis. In a right-handed person the left hemisphere is most often associated with logical thought, causal sequences and deductive reasoning. The right hemisphere is more often associated with the grasp of rhythms, spatial relationships and intuition (Ornstein, 1972). Gestalt is an approach which emphasises right-hemispheric, non-linear thinking – not at the expense of other ways of knowing but as a complement to these. Thinking with the right side of the brain applies the kind of intuition which can, for example, lead aware people to sense the emotional climate of the family as-a-whole from the atmosphere in its living room. A very tidy room with bare walls and functional furniture creates a different Gestalt from a softly upholstered room with pictures, flowers and space to sprawl.

The Gestaltist's approach is particularly characterised by the use of metaphor, fantasy and imagery, working with body posture and movement, enactment and visualisation, time distortion and the full expression of feelings involving the whole body in action.

> In summary, most of the techniques and procedures used by Gestalt therapists appear to disrupt left lobe functions and to evoke right lobe perception and memories in order to allow past and present experiences to be more adequately symbolised and integrated. (Fagan, 1977: 67)

Fritz Perls was the colourful and iconoclastic originator of Gestalt therapy. He rebelled against the analytic approach of the time (which he saw as reductionist, deterministic and over-intellectualising) to re-establish a balance in psychiatry. Often he would make provocative overstatements such as 'lose your mind and come to your senses', and he ridiculed intellectualisation by calling it 'bullshit'. People with outdated misconceptions of Gestalt sometimes still misunderstand such aphorisms to mean a complete replacement of the left hemispheric intellectual functions. Modern Gestalt aims for an integration of body, feelings and intellect, seeing the person's most basic needs within the context of the social environment.

Gestalt is also theoretically an integrative approach to counselling rooted in an existential orientation which combines psychoanalytic knowledge with procedural inventiveness through use of three primary devices – relationship, awareness and experiment.

For readers who want to understand the historical and philosophical roots of Gestalt before exploring its practical applications, here follows a broad explanation of the Gestalt approach and its theory in the context of the psychological movements of the twentieth century. Others may want to return to this chapter after reading the rest of the book, when the context may hold more meaning.

The Gestalt Approach in Context

The Gestalt approach originated in the existential-humanistic tradition of psychology. Practitioners sharing this viewpoint characteristically hold that it is impossible to engage in a counselling relationship without involving your values and your basic view of human nature. In this sense Gestalt is essentially a 'third force' humanistic psychology. It flowered in the 1950s and 1960s and grew to professional, theoretical and ethical maturity in the 1980s.

At one time the Gestalt approach had been cited as one of the most popular psychotherapeutic orientations in the United States (Polster and Polster, 1974). There are currently several hundred psychotherapists who primarily identify themselves as Gestalt therapists in Britain.

Gestalt therapy finds its roots in one of the three major streams of psychology which all originated around the turn of the twentieth century. Freud's theory of psychoanalysis came to represent one major stream of psychological thinking and psychotherapy, with his first major work, *The Interpretation of Dreams*, being published in 1900. Freudian and Kleinian psychoanalytic thinking tends to view human beings as biologically determined and motivated primarily by sexual and aggressive drives. For Freud, the purpose of psychoanalysis is exploration and understanding or analysis, not necessarily change.

The second major stream derives its theoretical lineage from Pavlov (1928), the Russian psychophysiologist who studied conditioned reflexes and other learning behaviours. Theoreticians and practitioners following in his footsteps are usually referred to as learning theorists, behaviour modification specialists or, latterly, cognitive-behaviour therapists.

In 1968 Abraham Maslow coined the term 'third force psychology' to distinguish the third grouping which did not originate from either the Freudian or Pavlovian tradition. Gestalt belongs here. This humanistic/existential tradition has as its intellectual and ideological grandfather the originator of psychodrama, Jakob Moreno. Moreno was arguably the first psychiatrist to put 'the patient' in a centrally responsible role in his own life drama, and he worked to empower the patient to do his or her own healing. Moreno was applying group psychotherapy with children based on humanistic existential principles and writing about it by 1908 (Moreno, 1979).

Eric Berne, the founder of transactional analysis (which is also an existential/humanistic psychotherapy), wrote a favourable review of *Gestalt Therapy Verbatim* by Perls (1969b). He highlighted the connection between Gestalt and psychodrama when he wrote:

> Dr. Perls is a learned man. He borrows from or encroaches upon pyschoanalysis, transactional analysis, and other systematic approaches. But he knows who he is and does not end up as an eclectic. In his selection of specific techniques, he shares with other 'active' psychotherapists the 'Moreno' problem: the fact that nearly all known 'active' techniques were first tried out by Dr. J. R. Moreno in psychodrama, so that it is difficult to come up with an original idea in this regard. (Berne, 1970: 163–4)

Fritz Perls himself identified Gestalt as one of three types of 'existential therapy' along with the Dasein therapy of Binswanger (1958) and the logotherapy of Frankl (1964/1969). However, Perls saw Gestalt as the only psychotherapy based purely on phenomenology – a psychological approach based on a philosophy which works away from concepts and towards pure awareness. In order to discover the meaning of an event, person or situation phenomenologists 'describe' experience, they do not interpret or prescribe it. Any judgement is perceived as clouding phenomenological perception and interfering with direct experience.

Many modern Gestalt theorists are of the opinion, even more than Perls realised, that Gestalt practice represents 'the most complete body of combined theory-technique which implements the major tenets of existentialism as they have application in the psychiatric situation' (Dublin, 1977: 134).

Historical Roots in Gestalt Psychology, Field Theory and Psychoanalysis

Gestalt Psychology

In 1926 Frederick (Fritz) Perls worked at the Institute for Brain-damaged Soldiers, founded by Dr Kurt Goldstein, an eminent neuropsychiatrist. Goldstein's stress on the organismic integrity of individual behaviour was a major psychological influence on the young Perls. Goldstein (1939) focused on the organismic integrity of individual behaviour and its drive towards *self-actualisation* no matter how damaged the organism may seem. Here Perls also became acquainted with the ideas of Gestalt psychology as articulated by Wertheimer (1944), Koffka (1935) and Köhler (1947/1970). Laura Perls, a Gestalt psychologist, was reputed to have been involved in his decision to change the name of his new therapy from 'concentration therapy' to 'Gestalt therapy'. She later became Fritz's wife and a leading exponent of Gestalt theory, practice and training in her own right. Throughout the major textbook *Gestalt Therapy: Excitement and Growth in the Human Personality* (Perls et al., 1951/1969) there are references to the *concentrating self* as being the core of the personality which seeks organismic self-actualisation.

The principles of Gestalt psychological theory were largely based on experiments in perception which emphasised the holistic, organismic and biological theory of human functioning and growth. Perls incorporated certain of these Gestalt psychology principles, such as the principle of figure and ground, the principle of closure, clear figure, the primary psychological need to create a meaningful personal construction out of the available field of impressions, and above all the human tendency to perceive wholes even where some of the information is missing in the system. 'The gestalt movement did exert a lasting influence on psychology by wounding mortally the tendency to "atomistic", building-block constructions, and by getting into the language of psychology the concept of "the organism-as-a-whole"' (Perls et al., 1951/1969: 26).

In Gestalt theory the central human activity is viewed as people's need to give *meaning* to their perceptions, their experience and their existence. The Gestalt approach is therefore concerned with defining the nature of human lives in terms of meaningful wholes, whether these be biological or spiritual. Most of Gestalt practice derived from Gestalt theory is based on an exploration of how such human needs arise, how they are frustrated, and how they are satisfied. The structure of this book is intended to reflect the process: it will elaborate identifiable phases of this process (Gestalt formation and destruction) in a characteristic cyclic pattern reflecting the possible developmental sequences in counselling.

One central Gestalt psychology paradigm for the emergence, prioritising and satiation of needs is the relationship between 'figure and ground'. This is the basic perceptual principle of making the wholes of human needs or experiences meaningful. This relationship is illustrated in Figure 1.1, which

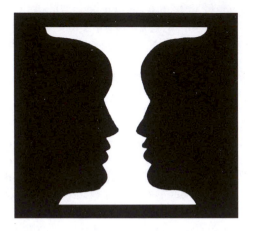

Figure 1.1   *Figure and ground*

can be seen as either two faces or one vase, but both cannot be perceived at the same moment. When the one is figure, the other is background, and vice-versa. For any individual the 'figure' is usually that which is most relevant or meaningful to the person, that which draws his or her interest in a dominant manner. In the absence of basic satisfactions, biological hungers such as needs for food or stimulation may be compelling figures determining the person's whole existential focus. For example, for a hungry Ethiopian, mere porridge would be a more complete and compelling figure than the aesthetic satisfaction which some privileged people may derive from 'nouvelle cuisine'! However, basic needs, such as sleep, can also be abrogated in service of higher needs; for example, traditional fasting over certain religious holidays.

'Ground' refers to the background of our figural experiences; for example, when I am paying attention to the letters on this page the music in the room is the 'background'. Of course by choosing to pay attention to the music, that may become foreground for me at that moment. The Gestalt approach emphasises that good experience is predicated upon the perception of one clear figure after another. A clear figure may be, for example, the biological need for sleep or a social need for intimacy. A good figure is one which is clear, sharply distinguished from the background and of strong interest. The changing pattern of a person's needs neither merge into one another, nor do they dominate the system once they have been met. When my need to sleep and rest has been met, I move forward with full energy and enthusiasm to my work. Having satiated my need for intellectual stimulation, I freely and completely engage with my friend in playful conversation.

Conceptually, the *sequence of moments* in the shift between figure and ground constitutes the so-called 'cycle of experience' or the Gestalt formation and destruction cycle. This way of describing what happens dynamically in the alternation between figure and ground will be discussed in detail later. The *process* of a figure/ground shift may occur slowly over years of training, as for example the need to qualify as a medical doctor. It may also occur in a matter of seconds as in the sudden 'aha' experience when a client suddenly integrates a new insight, such as a fundamental similarity between what he needed from his mother and what he continues to need from his wife. Such an insight may completely alter the relationship between past and future, expectation and understanding, figure and ground.

The process of moving flexibly and creatively between figure and ground can be chronically or traumatically interrupted. Either rigidity (fixation) or lack of clear figure formation (fickleness) interferes with the natural completion of an adequate Gestalt. This results in a 'fixed Gestalt' or an 'unfinished experience/situation' which interferes with good contact with self, others, or the environment in the present. Then the unmet needs become incomplete Gestalten which demand attention and prevent the formation of new Gestalten.

Researchers in Gestalt psychology, such as Zeigarnik (1927) and Ovsiankina (1928), documented the psychological tension which accompanies experiences which are incomplete or unresolved and the human need to attempt to close these 'unfinished situations'. According to investigators such as Whyte (1954) incomplete patterns (for example, crystalline faces) in nature are trying to become complete. The mathematical symbolism of patterns also displays a tendency of movement either towards completeness or disintegration. Most people are familiar with the kind of nagging discomfort associated with an uncompleted task such as a half-written letter or an undelivered retort.

There is an apocryphal story of a famous composer (sometimes Mozart, sometimes Beethoven) who tried but could not go to sleep because someone had played a concerto on the piano downstairs without completing the final chords. The composer could not rest until he had been downstairs and played the closing bars himself. Having thus 'finished' the incomplete auditory Gestalt, he had a peaceful night's rest.

On a visual or perceptual level this tendency is demonstrated by our need to complete Figure 1.2 in a meaningful way. Counselling deals with such 'unfinished business' in people's lives by removing the impositions, distortions or interruptions to the formation of vital, meaningful and fulfilling figure-ground experiences in everyday life. Of course, all of us can tolerate a certain level of unfinished business, but when these interruptions become chronic or overwhelming, temporary or permanent disability may result. This is the field of the Gestalt practitioner's endeavour.

Figure 1.2   *An incomplete Gestalt*

Unresolved childhood situations are often experienced as 'unfinished situations' or 'incompletely formed Gestalten'. These unfinished situations continue to disturb the person in adult life. They tend to interfere with behaviours, perceptions and thinking related to effective functioning in the here-and-now. This interference 'binds' psychological energy and drains it away from effective functioning in the current reality. Pathology may be caused when an unfinished or incomplete Gestalt is inappropriately or prematurely 'closed' under stress. This closure may take physiological, affective, cognitive or behavioural form. For example, when the parents divorce and it is not sufficiently explained to the child, Johnny experiences the tension of an incomplete Gestalt. Because he needs to give meaning to his experience, he may decide with his three-year-old logic that his parents split up because he was not born a girl. This would be an example of inappropriate cognitive closure. For the child it *was* appropriate at the time, since it made sense or meaning out of his existence then. It becomes inappropriate, however, when the thirty-year-old man still experiences at some level of awareness that he is of the 'wrong sex'.

Field Theory

Kurt Lewin (1952), a German psychologist, was the founder of Field Theory in psychology. From him, Perls learnt to view psychological relationships in terms of the surrounding field. Lewin postulated that it is impossible to view a person except in the context of his or her environmental field. This interrelationship of the person with the environment is a central tenet of the Gestalt approach. Lewin was convinced that behaviour was determined by the psychological present (the here-and-now) more than by the past or the future. He considered 'the unconscious' to be that which was not figural at the moment.

From this perspective, human beings can be understood only within the system of which they are a significant component part. A Gestaltist would always work within the matrix of the *person* with *needs* in a sociocultural *context*. Of course this means that the observer (or practitioner) is always part of this interactional field, and attempts to claim 'neutrality' or 'objectivity' or to study the psychology of the individual in isolation are unscientific, seriously incomplete and ultimately limited. 'Only the interplay of organism and environment ... constitutes the psychological situation, not the organism and environment taken separately' (Perls et al., 1951/1969: xii). In this way, Gestalt is one of the earliest psychotherapeutic approaches to incorporate a *systems perspective* on human problems.

In some psychoanalytic theories the person is often referred to in terms of object-relations. In Gestalt, organism and organismic (after Goldstein) are the terms most frequently used to refer to the person. This is to emphasise the dynamic nature of people as biological beings (with animal, social and spiritual needs) systematically interdependent with their environment – a truly ecological approach. Zinker, for example, considers 'that most characteristics of psychological systems are virtually identical to those of psychological fields and of psychological gestalten' (1987: 76).

Friedlaender and Holism

During his time in South Africa, where he founded the psychoanalytic institute, Perls was also influenced by the writings of Jan Smuts, the then Prime Minister. Jan Smuts developed the concept of holism which extends to a radical acceptance of body–mind unity which is not based on any notion of causality (Smuts, 1926). An holistic approach to the person embraces and affirms complexity, inclusion and diversity and resists reductionism.

Another major influence on Gestalt theory was the ideas of Friedlaender, who wrote the book *Schöpferische Indifferenz (Creative Indifference)* (1918). Friedlaender considered that thinking in opposites is an essential quality of human mentality and of life itself. He posited that opposites within the same contexts such as sadism/masochism, energy/lassitude are more closely related to each other than to any other concept. This explains the human capacity for subtle differentiation of degrees within the range between the opposites. In Gestalt practice a point of 'creative indifference' is frequently sought. This is an attitude of interest balanced almost equally between the two contrasting poles of, for example, disappointment and fulfilled expectation. A counsellor who uses the Gestalt approach is equally interested in both poles of the client's experience and may at times seek to cultivate a similar attitude of 'neutral interest' in the client with regard to his or her own psychological process. 'By remaining alert in the centre, we can acquire a creative ability . . . By avoiding a one-sided outlook we gain a much deeper insight into the structure and function of the organism' (Perls, 1969a: 15). In this way the paradoxical relationship of apparent polarities becomes more obvious. This ease with paradox, simultaneous truths and apparent contradictions pervades Gestalt practice. Suffice it for now to say that Gestalt as a therapeutic approach today fits most comfortably with the discoveries and perspectives of modern physics (Capra, 1976/1978) and complexity science (Briggs and Peat, 1990).

Psychoanalytic Revisions

Perls made major revisions to Freudian theory, including a particular emphasis on the oral developmental phases in children. Drawing from his psychoanalytic training, Perls used the oral, anal, genital developmental sequence developed by Freud as ground for much of his clinical work. He certainly assumed a knowledge of psychoanalysis in his writings. He contributed an original elaboration of the hunger instinct in infantile development and he frequently drew analogies with mental metabolism. The manner in which one relates to new information, for example, gulping it up, frequently mirrors one's relationship with food.

He distinguished between the *prenatal (before-birth) stage* and the *pre-dental (suckling) stage*. The suckling phase is characterised by the 'hanging-on bite' of the infant. The conscious active task of the newly born child is to incorporate food – its mother's milk.

In the next phase, which can be called the *incisor or biting phase*, the baby's front teeth erupt. These front teeth are used as scissors, also now involving the use of the jaw muscles to destroy the food's gross structure. As an infant bites, its mother may experience pain, and biting can become identified with hurting and being hurt: 'The more the activity of biting is inhibited, the less will such a child develop the ability to tackle an object, if and when the situation calls for it' (Perls, 1969a: 109). The infant cannot repress the impulse to bite without compromising her need for a satisfying source of food. In the fourth phase the molars come into their own for the tasks of *biting and chewing*, grinding the food mechanically into a pulp ready for metabolising by digestive juices.

Perls drew many analogies throughout his work between eating behaviour and psychological life. For example, an inhibition of the biologically appropriate destructive action of the teeth may later manifest in harmful ways such as killing, cruelty, warring or self-torture and suicide (Perls, 1969a: 110). 'The terms destruction, aggression, hatred, rage and sadism are used in psychoanalytical literature almost as synonyms, and one never knows definitely whether reference is made to an emotion, to a function, or to a perversion' (Perls, 1969a: 117).

Perls conceptualised aggression in terms of its original root of 'to reach out', and wished to re-establish its true biological function (which is not senseless discharge) but rather application of one's will to bring about relevant changes in one's environment.

Perls disagreed with Freud's view of the mental apparatus as divided into ego, id and superego. Perls thought it more constructive to consider one whole self which functioned in particular ways. Perls argued that mental constructs of divisions inside the personality encouraged splits in the personality (Yontef, 1979a: 54).

Perls stressed the wholeness or integrity of the personality and viewed the ego as the here-and-now experience of the person. Gestalt focuses on the here-and-now, not the there-and-then; life is to be lived, not only talked about. Some misconceptions about Gestalt hold that Gestalt therefore does not deal with the client's past or historical accounts. Gestalt practice does not mean the exclusion of remembering, imagining and planning as functions of the present. However psychoanalysis makes the *past* foreground, Gestalt makes the *present* foreground (Clarkson, 1988).

Perls also disagreed with Freud's view of the super-ego as the source of anxiety in the form of references to the 'seething cauldron of anti-social id wishes'. For Perls, 'anxiety is the tension between the now and the later' (Perls, 1976). He adds that excitement without creative expression causes anxiety, and as such is to be avoided. Excitement is the life force and is positively valued in marshalling the person into action to satisfy his needs. Any disturbances in people's excitement metabolism diminishes their vitality.

Gestalt therapy (like existential analysis) certainly rejects the notion of a region of the human mind which is permanently or practically inaccessible to awareness.

> Perls does not use the term 'the unconscious' in the way that Freud did. This is not meant to be construed as a denial of experiences that are out of awareness. Perls has a different perspective on the phenomenon of processes which are not conscious. (Clarkson, 1988: 78)

The concept of the unconscious as an inaccessible region within the personality is replaced in Gestalt therapy by the shifting figure/ground of the functional concept of 'awareness'.

> And therefore, rather than talking of the unconscious, we prefer to talk about the *at-this-moment-unaware*. This term is much broader and wider than the term 'unconscious'. This unawareness contains not only repressed material, but material which never came into awareness, and material which has faded or has been assimilated or has been built into larger gestalts. The unaware includes skills, patterns of behaviour, motoric and verbal habits, blind spots, etc. (Perls, 1976: 54)

Wilhelm Reich (1972) was one of Perls's analysts. From him, Perls integrated the manifestations of skeletal and muscular armour in chronic character disturbances as the end-result of unresolved emotional conflicts. Reich discovered that people 'store' their emotional memories and their defences against these in their muscles and internal organs, as well as their emotional memories and their defences against these. Such physiological restrictions can be considered as a premature physiological closure of a traumatic experience; vaginismus in a woman who was sexually assaulted as a child is an example. Gestalt approaches, therefore, focus attention on the 'sensing body' as a major route to psychological integration and a release of free energy. (Of course integration is never finally achieved; nor is the process of maturation ever completed.)

Perls's other analyst, Karen Horney, might have provided the seeds for some of his subsequent ideas about topdog/underdog through her awareness of 'the tyranny of the shoulds' (Horney, 1937/1977).

Finally, it should be remembered that the early Gestalt therapists had a very thorough grounding in psychoanalytic practice, and wrote taking for granted that readers were as familiar with the works of Freud, Reich, Rank and others as they were. Certain psychoanalytic contributions still pervade the clinical use of Gestalt, and modern Gestaltists are actively incorporating object-relations theory and self-theories (Yontef, 1988). Whether this dilutes Gestalt or, from psychoanalysis, adds to it is a point of dispute.

Transpersonal Elements (the 'Soul' in Gestalt)

Gestaltists have almost always found it important to acknowledge the transpersonal aspects of the meaning-giving endeavours of people within whatever idiom may be used. An approach which strives to deal with the whole person must take seriously the social need for religious experience however the individual defines his or her need for coherence. Modern Gestaltists such as Naranjo (1982) and Polster and Polster (1977) also value and include spiritual dimensions as part of the whole of psychological growth, change and development. Some Gestaltists have found great compatibility, if not identity, between Jungian concepts and Gestalt (Whitmont and Kaufmann, 1977; and Clarkson, 1989).

Zen was an important influence on early Gestalt theory. It is a Buddhist spiritual tradition which emphasises the attainment of enlightenment through direct, intuitive perception. It is very much a right hemispheric approach to understanding and may also, like Gestalt, *appear* anti-intellectual. However, such an interpretation would be very superficial. Zen does not focus on rationalistic intellectualisation, neither does it focus on passive, meditational quietude. Anecdotes, stories, poems, paradoxes and riddles are used as experiential vehicles towards enlightenment. These stories attempt to bypass cumbersome, logical intellectualisation which can impede genuine insight. The aim of these illustrations is:

> to precipitate some type of sudden realisation in the questioner's mind, or to test the depth of his insight. For this reason, such anecdotes cannot be 'explained' without spoiling their effect. In some respects they are like jokes

> which do not produce their intended effect of laughter when the 'punch line' requires further explanation. One must see the point immediately or not at all. (Watts, 1962/1974: 107)

The moment of realisation or insight is neither purely rational nor purely intuitive, but it is an integration of *both* with experience. In this way it resembles the moment of therapeutic insight when people suddenly get a new realisation (an 'aha' experience) which transforms their way of being in the world. Gestalt experiments are not based on Zen but resemble it in practice. Gestaltists often provide growth-provoking 'puzzles' which might only be solved by the whole person with right and left hemisphere functions grounded in experience. Because Gestalt so needs *direct* experience in order to come alive as an approach, and the written word can be so limiting, I will intersperse some Zen stories at various points throughout the book. Hopefully the Zen mondo will also serve to remind the reader repeatedly of the paradoxical nature of the Gestalt approach. As in human life, often apparent contradictions merely shadow one truth. Gestalt welcomes paradox knowing that by truly staying where one is, already one is changing.

Philosophical Assumptions of the Gestalt Approach

Among approaches to counselling, Gestalt is particularly richly grounded in important philosophical roots. Obviously in an introductory text such as this only some aspects can be highlighted, but readers are invited to study the source books in the reference lists and pursue the connections between theory, practice and values for themselves.

Existence Precedes Essence

For existentialists the notion of 'existential choice' is fundamental to being human. This means that each of us is choosing what we accept, reject, think, feel or how we behave. 'Awareness of and responsibility for the total field, for the self as well as the other, these give meaning and pattern to the individual's life' (Perls, 1976: 49).

This responsibility can be avoided only at the price of being in 'bad faith' or, in person-centred terms, 'inauthentic' or 'incongruent'. An example is the use of language which presupposes a passive victim orientation to life,

'I have to pay my taxes or do my washing' is replaced by 'I choose to do these things because I do not want the consequence of other choices'. This stresses the inevitable responsibility of every human being for the choices that he or she makes.

With this assumption of awareness and responsibility, increased response-ability becomes possible. This means that the more fully I can become aware of who I am and what I am doing at this moment, the more freedom I can experience to change and the more I am able to choose my responses. For example, choosing in full awareness an act of self-sacrifice can change an act of compulsive masochism into an authentic act of good faith. Of course there are many situations where people do not have many choices, such as prison, poverty or privation. According to an existentialist vision (Frankl, 1964/1969), they are still able to choose their responses to such situations. We are indeed condemned to freedom (Sartre, 1948). For me Gestalt practice represents a complete body of theory and technique which appears to use the major tenets of existentialism in the counselling and psychotherapeutic situation.

The Phenomenon is Primary

Yontef (1979b) describes Gestalt therapy as clinical phenomenology. Phenomenology, as developed by Husserl (1970), Sartre (1948) and Merleau-Ponty (1973), is the philosophical approach which is at the very heart of Gestalt. Perls indeed saw Gestalt as the only therapy based on purely phenomenological principles. Phenomenology seeks the truth or source of knowledge by concentrating on immediate experience, shorn of assumptions or presuppositions.

The philosophical assumptions of Gestalt emphasise the primacy of the world of immediate experience, that is to say, my individual and unique experience precedes any attempt at labelling or categorisation or judgement. Phenomenon in this sense is the 'immediate object of perception' (Onions, 1973: 1569). The phenomenological method which pays total attention to the phenomenon (person, experience or object) as it presents itself, becomes the method of choice in the counselling approach. Perls called Gestalt the therapy of the 'obvious'. Description is considered more important than interpretation. Clients are enabled to find *their own meaning* through this process. For example, a client was concerned that people repeatedly experienced him as giving them double messages consisting of 'come close' and 'stay away I don't trust you'. It was only when the Gestalt practitioner drew attention to the fact that one side of his mouth was obviously damaged that he felt released to speak about the traumatic incident involving a betrayal of trust which caused the injury.

Its phenomenological orientation implies a disciplined focus on experiencing what is obvious in a given situation without prejudgements or expectations. In common with phenomenological philosophers, Gestalt theorists emphasise that the person can only be understood in terms of an intentional relationship with the world (place) and that experience is physical (body) in a temporal frame of reference (time).

Finally, the sociality of our experience and behaviour is another phenomenologically essential feature of human existence. People cannot be understood outside of the context of their ongoing relationships with other people or separate from their interconnectedness with the world. No individual can be considered free within an oppressive *system*. For example, Sartre (1948) points out that 'I cannot make liberty my aim unless I make that of others equal in my aim' (p. 52).

Summary

Passons (1975) summarises these assumptions about using the Gestalt approach to counselling as follows:

1   A person is a whole and is (rather than has) a body, emotions, thoughts, sensations and perceptions – all of which function interrelatedly.
2   A person is part of his or her environment and cannot be understood apart from it.
3   People are proactive rather than reactive. They determine their own responses to the world.
4   People are capable of being aware of their sensations, thoughts, emotions and perceptions.
5   People, through self-awareness, are capable of choice and therefore responsible for their behaviour.
6   People possess the potential and resources to live effectively and to satisfy their needs.
7   People can experience themselves only in the present.
8   The past and the future can be experienced only in the now through remembering and anticipating.
9   People are neither intrinsically good nor bad.

In short, Gestalt as an approach to counselling and psychotherapy can be compared to a tree. It has its roots in psychoanalysis and character analysis, its trunk is phenomenology and existentialism and its branches reach up towards eastern philosophy and transpersonal understandings. The tree stands in a landscape of holism and field theory with which it is inextricably interlinked. At its heart is the central appreciation of being: *Physis* or the *élan vital*, (see Clarkson 1991, 1997).

> Now normally the *élan vital*, the life force energizes by sensing, by listening, by scouting, by describing the world – how is the world there. Now this life force apparently first mobilizes the center – *if* you have a center. And the center of the personality is what used to be called the soul: the emotions, the feelings, the spirit. (Perls 1969b: 63)

The next chapter will discuss more specifically how the historical, psychological and philosophical roots of Gestalt have become fundamentals of the Gestalt approach to counselling.

2

FUNDAMENTALS OF THE GESTALT
APPROACH TO COUNSELLING

Tanzan and Ekido, two Zen monks, were travelling companions on a muddy road during a storm. On their way they met a lovely young girl in a silk kimono who was unable to cross the intersection. Tanzan lifted her in his arms and carried her over the mud putting her down on the other side. Many hours later in the lodging temple Ekido confronted Tanzan. He said 'We monks are not meant to go near women. To carry such a young and lovely one was wrong. Why did you do that?' Tanzan replied: 'I left the girl there . . . Are you still carrying her?'

(Reps, 1971: 28)

The Therapeutic Relationship

Gestalt practitioners affirm the primary values of the living existential encounter between two real human beings, both of whom are risking themselves in the dialogue of the healing process. The central focus is the moment-by-moment process of the relationship between the client and the counsellor. In this encounter, the goal is a full and complete authentic meeting between these two people. (Naturally such a meeting may include each experiencing existential separation and essential aloneness.) The development of the *capacity* for genuine relationship forms the core of the healing process and has been described by Hycner (1985) as a relationship basically characterised by dialogue – a *dialogic relationship*.

As they work through the many stage-posts of their journey, the client gains emotional resources, security and freedom, and the counsellor comes to be seen more and more as a 'real' person. No longer is the counsellor experienced merely as a projective substitute for figures from the past, and no longer are past patterns habitually used in the present.

Laura Perls has mentioned 'that she was profoundly influenced by a personal meeting with Martin Buber, and that the true essence of Gestalt therapy was the relationship formed between therapist and client' (Hycner, 1985: 27). Buber described this 'I–You' ('Ich und Du' in German) relationship as a genuine meeting between two unique people in which both openly respect the essential humanity of the other. Buber (1958/1984) writes that there are two primary human attitudes, the 'I–You' relationship and the 'I–It' relationship. The 'I–It' relationship occurs when we turn others into objects. An actual example of the latter occurs when women and children are turned into pornographic objects for 'use'. Symbolically, this may occur when clients and counsellors 'use' each other as mere 'objects' for projection or analysis without duly honouring the essential humanity of their relationship. Gestalt recognises that from the first encounter onwards, client and counsellor exchange many moments of recognition of each other's real humanity. It is here that there is the most fertile ground for Gestalt work. From the very beginning both participants engage in a relationship of mutuality where not only the client is changed by the counsellor, but the counsellor is also affected and changed by the client. Ultimately, it is only in the context of an authentic relationship that the uniqueness of the individual can be truly recognised. In the recognition and acceptance of who he is, paradoxically productive change can become possible. Every moment is created anew.

Wholeness

A cornerstone of the Gestalt approach is its emphasis on the wholeness of the person in the counselling relationship, not just the intrapsychic or merely the interpersonal dimension. In the counselling process different aspects of a person may be emphasised at different times. These will probably include symbolic, behavioural, physiological, affective, cognitive and spiritual aspects of the client's life. The counsellor, however, will always have as a guiding principle the integration of all the many facets of that unique individual. The acceptance and celebration of this multi-dimensional wholeness is also considered a possible goal for the client. This is not 'imposed upon' the client, but is based on a belief that human beings want to experience their wholeness, individual richness and integration of diversity.

The Gestalt approach is essentially realistic and integrative because it takes into account both the dark and regressive aspects of being human and also of our innate strivings towards health, happiness and self-actualisation. Gestalt does not deny the irrational roots of hatred, envy and fear at individual and collective levels. In this sense it seeks to actualise and celebrate life in *all* its varied richness. Interestingly enough Goodman (co-author of *Gestalt Therapy: Excitement and Growth in the Human Personality* (Perls et al., 1951/1969)), one of the founders of the Gestalt approach, was an anarchist and a questioning, iconoclastic and challenging spirit lives on in modern Gestalt.

A Gestalt-oriented approach to counselling is based on the absolute inseparable unity of bodily experience, emotions, language, ethics, rationality, meaning-making and spirituality (whether or not in awareness) (see Clarkson, 1975; 2002a). Gestalt has as its fulcrum the existential invitation to the client to *be* himself or herself as fully and completely as possible. The client becomes his or her body. Physical expressiveness or bodily movement comes naturally to client and counsellor in the Gestalt approach. It is not considered that I just 'get' a cold or asthma, nor that my unhappiness 'causes' my asthma. Neither does my cold 'cause' my depression. In a fundamental way my body/mind self is reacting as a whole. This does *not* mean that you are to blame for your cancer; it does mean that I am 'response-able'. Accepting in this way that the person is a unity of psyche and soma, Gestalt practitioners emphasise that people can take responsibility and be active in their own healing processes.

> If the coronary of a heart is hardened, excitement leads to, amongst other prominent symptoms, attacks of anxiety. On the other hand an attack of anxiety on a person with a healthy heart is identical with certain physiological changes in the function of the heart and breathing apparatus. An anxiety attack without breathing difficulties, quickening of the pulse and similar symptoms does not exist.
>
> No emotion, like rage, sadness, shame or disgust occurs without its physiological as well as its psychological components coming into play. (Perls, 1969a: 33)

For Perls, as well as for many modern Gestaltists, body and psyche are identical, denoting two aspects of the same phenomenon. The capacity of the Gestalt approach to transcend limiting notions of body–mind duality and linear causality is unparalleled amongst counselling approaches, and potentially offers an enormous contribution to the field of psychosomatics.

Illness is seen as a disturbance in the organism's natural tendency to regulate the self.

Self-regulation

In Gestalt a person is seen as having a natural or organismic tendency to regulate the self. Perls considered the *self* as the function of contacting the actual transient present, and saw ego, id, and personality as separate partial structures of appearances of the self, mistaken for the whole function of the self. 'Self' he defined as the system of awareness at the boundary between self and that which is not the self. It is also the evaluation of this process. 'Self exists where there are the shifting boundaries of contact . . . Wherever there is a boundary and contact occurs, it is, in so far, creative self' (Perls et al., 1951/1969: 374). It is spontaneous and engaged with its forming Gestalten in a vividly experienced way. Perls also conceptualised it as ground of action and passion – the actualisation of the potential. In this creative aspect it may be the 'concentrating self' – conscious of itself and its processes, or it may operate without the individual being conscious of the processes of emotion, evaluation and integration of organic needs.

In order to grow and develop people strive to maintain a balance between need gratification and tension elimination. Gestalt is a need-based approach. By stressing needs it places a very important focus on motivation which is lacking in many other approaches to psychotherapy. It assumes that whenever an imbalance occurs within the person, or in relation to the environment, this imbalance will be experienced as a dominant figure against the background of that person's other experiences. The healthy person differentiates this meaningful need and responds to it appropriately, thereby restoring the balance, releasing new energy and allowing the next important need (Gestalt) to emerge.

Effective self-regulation depends on a discriminating sensory awareness which allows the person to use what is nourishing to him or her (in terms, for example, of food, people, stimulus) and to reject what is not nourishing. Through the use of aggression (a value-free Gestalt term which connotes the life force) a person can destroy or 'destructure' food, experiences or jigsaw puzzles in order to flourish, grow or play more enjoyably. The cyclical nature of this self-regulating process will be discussed in Chapter 3.

Working from their knowledge of the organism's tendency to self-regulation, Gestaltists assume that people know at some level what is good for them. There is some research evidence that untraumatised infants naturally select a balanced diet in terms of their individual needs if given sufficient choices (Cannon, 1932). This organismic self-regulation, if left undisturbed, usually leads towards a healthy, balanced and self-actualising outcome. The goal of counselling is to re-establish this natural and healthy functioning – the most authentic connection with their *élan vital* (physis).

From this perspective people who come for counselling are those who have experienced some interruption or distortion of this healthy self-regulating process. What was originally a child's healthy withdrawal from a punitive parent figure becomes solidified as an incapacitating social shyness in the chronological adult. The organismic goal would be to re-establish satisfying approach behaviour towards potentially friendly people while retaining the ability to withdraw; however, to do so in a discriminating way which is relevant to here-and-now reality.

The Attitude of the Counsellor

To practise the Gestalt approach means that the counsellor uses himself or herself actively and authentically in the encounter with the other person. It is more a 'way of being and doing' than a set of techniques or a prescribed formula for counselling. Gestalt is characterised by a willingness on the part of the counsellor to be active, present as a person and interventionist in the counselling relationship. This is based on the assumption that treating the client as a human being with intelligence, responsibility and active choices at any moment in time is most likely to invite the client into autonomy, self-healing and integration.

There is research evidence that schoolchildren and students respond differentially to their teachers' unvoiced expectations of them (Rosenthal and Jacobson, 1968). When teachers believed children were unintelligent and could not learn, the children responded with lowered performance, no matter what their original gifts. Positive expectations influenced the students' performance in positive ways. There may be a lesson for psychotherapists: expect resistance and investment in the *status quo* and those phenomena are more likely to recur. Perhaps our expectations of positive growth, willingness to risk and take responsibility in our clients may enhance the likelihood that they would manifest these qualities in counselling and in life.

The Gestalt approach values a commitment to experimentation, creativity and risk-taking for both client and counsellor. Client and counsellor engage in developing new experiments and creating *experiments* of doing, being and behaving. The client is an active partner in the experiment and the counsellor is ideally willing and able to participate in an experience about which neither can predict the outcome. The process of Gestalt counselling at its best provides experiences of how life can be fully and richly lived. This achievable ideal is characterised by acute sensory awareness, a range of emotional responses and effective action. A client reports 'I see colours more vividly now than I ever have before. I didn't know the world was so richly patterned.' Another client reports 'Not only am I happy a lot of the time, I also experience my sadness and loss with greater intensity and have discovered that I have infinite variations of irritation, annoyance and anger.'

The Place of Technique in Gestalt Counselling

The Gestalt approach to counselling can embrace a wide variety of diverse but specific techniques within an holistic frame of reference which integrates mind and body, action and introspection. Techniques are not prescribed, but Gestalt practitioners are encouraged to invent appropriate 'experiments' which invite people into heightened experience of the body–mind self, authentic encounters with meaningful others, and an impactful relationship with the environment. The richness of technique in Gestalt is constrained only by the personal limitations of imagination, intellect or responsiveness of individual counsellors or clients. Interventions to facilitate the goals of Gestalt will be described later in the book using case examples as illustrations to emphasise how techniques have to be rediscovered and re-invented for each client at different stages in the relationship. At no point are these intended to be prescriptive, exclusive or even helpful when used out of context or divorced from the moment-by-moment flow between each unique counsellor/client partnership. They are tentatively shared here in this format to provoke practitioners to their own discoveries, not to pre-empt such effort. Mechanical use of techniques at selected stages of counselling (merely crystallised for ease of communication and publication in this book) is antithetical to the very spirit of Gestalt. Yet if Gestalt is to become communicable and comparable with other approaches, perhaps even this risk of misunderstanding should be taken.

Some approaches to counselling depend on 'withholding' the real person of the counsellor from the therapeutic encounter. Any fixed attitude such as this is anathema to Gestalt. Gestalt makes the dialogue between the two partners in growth the central healing dimension. This demands considerable awareness, self-knowledge and responsibility from the counsellor. It also means that 'technique' is secondary to the therapeutic relationship. According to Resnick:

> every Gestalt therapist could stop doing any Gestalt technique that had ever been done and go right on doing Gestalt therapy. If they couldn't, then they weren't doing Gestalt therapy in the first place. They were fooling around with a bag of tricks and a bunch of gimmicks. (1984: 19)

Experimentation within the relationship will probably always be a characteristic of Gestalt. In fact Gestalt has been defined as the permission to be creative (Zinker, 1978). Most current Gestalt approaches are not invasive of the client's integrity in the way that was sometimes practised in the past. In practice the greatest respect is accorded to the relationship between two whole people. Most modern Gestaltists would adopt a therapeutic relationship characterised by dialogue rather than invasion or deprivation. The Gestalt approach emphasises the widest possible range of openness, flexibility *and* structure, depending on the needs of each particular moment in the healing process.

Psychosomatic Unity

The counselling encounter is not only verbal but involves all the other ways in which a person continually interacts with a given environment. Most obviously this involves 'body language'. For example, by deliberately intensifying the tension, Daisy discovers that 'the pain in my neck' is a physiological enactment of her daughter being 'a pain in the neck'. An apparently meaningless kicking movement of a foot, when focused upon, expresses the client's irritation at the counsellor's head-nodding mannerism.

In Gestalt (true to the phenomenological values of observation, description and discovery) such patterns are usually *not* interpreted. The client is invited by means of creative experimentation to discover his meanings for himself. A person who habitually walks with a caved-in chest and rounded shoulders continues to enact in the present the beaten-up little boy of the past, while at the same time signalling to the environment that he is the kind of person who 'gets beaten up'. Frequently people in the environment will respond out of awareness to these non-verbal cues and provide recurrences of the original trauma. Quite often muggers, and even commonplace bullies, seem to have an ability to pick upon these non-verbal signs and act accordingly. And so the original trauma is repeated. However, by imbuing his body and his life experiences with awareness, choice becomes possible for a person.

Demands on the Counsellor

The counsellor needs to be willing to develop all of her potentialities in order to be authentic when she invites the client to develop all of the client's potentialities. Because Gestalt counsellors as people need to be so transparent, they cannot hide behind a 'professional mask' or 'objective role'. Not only personal psychotherapy, but a passionate commitment to lifelong growth and personal development is therefore essential. Gestalt is not a 'technique' that can be used only in the consulting room. It demands from the counsellor a way of life compatible with its values – a willingness to be open to the exigencies of existence. Excitement is positively valued as is vividness and richness of experience. Adjustment to limitations imposed by society that are injurious to growth (for example, keeping a stiff upper lip at a funeral) or 'acceptance of the *status quo*' are considered to be anti-therapeutic and stultifying.

Respect for the Integrity of Defence and Challenge to Change

Gestalt practice requires and facilitates the courage to face existential risk and disappointment while ever remaining hopeful of human growth and development. Seeking the unexpected and the new, while using the supportive structures of the past, is characteristic of good Gestalt counselling.

> The reorganising of the personality consists of both disintegrating and integrating processes, and should be balanced so that only such amount of dissociated material should be set free as the patient is capable of assimilating.

Otherwise his social or even biological function may be dangerously upset. (Perls, 1979: 21)

The counsellor provides for each individual client a 'safe emergency'. Too much support can deprive the client of the opportunity to grow through frustration. Too much challenge can be invasive and sadistic. Allowing the client to repeat in counselling endlessly the processes she habitually uses to substitute for genuine feeling, experience and action can also be ultimately destructive. Yet at any one time with any one client provocative challenge, nurturing support or laissez-faire neutrality may be the modality of choice.

Dynah, a sensual intelligent middle-aged client, experiments with wearing bright and vivid colours to accentuate her willingness 'to be seen as a colourful and interesting person'. Yet she also retains the comforting and healthy caring qualities which sustained her family through years of child-rearing.

The Place of Diagnosis in Gestalt

Historically the Gestalt approach has been viewed as anti-diagnostic in the sense that each person is considered as a unique and complete body–mind Gestalt. Rote labelling in terms of diagnoses or psychopathology represents a fragmentation of this inherent unity and individuality. Gestaltists have traditionally rejected such a dehumanisation of patients. To label people 'anal-retentive' or 'manic-depressive' can be to strip them of the unique ways in which they have chosen to give meaning to their existence in their historical context. Recognition of repeating patterns in human behaviour (whether momentary or long-term) is, however, intrinsic to an holistic approach.

Allowing for the danger of this kind of reductionism, Gestaltists do not invalidate a commitment to the recognition of repetitive self-destructive patterns of behaviour. Thus a person may be described as 'a person who habitually deflects or disrupts intimate contact', but this is a behavioural description allowing for permanent revision at any moment and *not* a way of categorising the person. From an holistic perception of the field, pattern can only coexist with potential disruption of the pattern. Modern Gestalt practitioners value, use and teach diagnostic schemes which are based on Gestalt descriptions as well as more conventional clinical diagnoses

(Delisle, 1988; Resnick, 1984; Van Dusen, 1975a; Yontef, 1984, 1987; Zinker, 1978).

The Here-and-now

In the past Gestalt has also mistakenly been seen as an anti-historical approach. Early emphasis on 'here-and-now' interactions was a pendulum reaction to the passive, non-involved psychoanalysis against which Fritz Perls rebelled. 'It seeks to transform that which is merely history or narrative into pungent, expressive action. Though aware participation in the present moment may include the remembering of something from one's past, it must be remembered with the fresh, felt poignancy that brings it indelibly into the present' (Polster and Polster, 1977).

Yontef (1988) contributed a particular extension of Gestalt phenomenological horizons by drawing attention to four space–time zones, all necessary to a therapeutic approach which is suitable for long-term work as well as short-term counselling or episodic interventions.

The familiar here-and-now time–space zone refers to the whole person environment field at any particular moment, including fantasies and plans about the future and memories and experiences about the past, relived in the freshness of 'the now'.

The person's 'life-space' constitutes the 'there-and-now' zone which includes the person's current existence – his or her real life – both in the counselling relationship and outside of it.

Thirdly, Yontef identifies the 'here-and-then', the *therapeutic context*, which particularly refers to the centrality of the therapeutic relationship, its continuity and its history as well as to other contexts which influence this relationship – such as referring agencies.

The fourth time–space zone is the 'there-and-then', the patient's life story, without which there can be no appreciation of how a person developed over time. This is the historical background that allows meaning to emerge, 'the sequence of prior experimental moments'.

Most current Gestaltists acknowledge that the past is indeed inherent in the present, and that movement over time is inseparable from a process theory. It is from this ground that the developmental phases of counselling over time form the spinal structure of this book.

Responsibility

The Gestalt approach is profoundly based on the notion that each person is responsible for the experience of his or her own life. This implies that every moment the individual makes choices to act – or not to act – in certain ways, and that he or she is responsible for all these choices. Viktor Frankl was a Jewish psychiatrist who survived several Nazi concentration camps to become one of the great existentialist psychotherapists of our time. According to Frankl (1964/1969), even when we are not personally responsible for the circumstances in which we find ourselves (such as a German concentration camp), we are still responsible for the meaning we give to our lives as we choose our attitudes towards, and our behaviour in, such situations.

Perls took this position to a radical extreme in the famous Gestalt prayer:

> I do my thing and you do your thing.
> I am not in this world to live up to your expectations
> – And you are not in this world to live up to mine,
>   You are you and I am I,
> If by chance we find each other, it's beautiful.
>   If not, it can't be helped. (Perls, 1969b: 4)

Modern Gestalt psychotherapy and counselling has moved beyond the hedonistic 'Perlsian' over-reactions which emphasised responsibility for the self over and against responsibility for others (Dublin, 1977).

Currently there is increasing recognition of the philosophical and *ecological* fact that responsibility for the self inevitably includes responsibility for the others who share our world. In this way, as well as in many others, Gestalt is a true systems approach. Gestalt is founded on the fact that content belongs in a context. No self can be separate from its environment. A client recently reported: 'When I first came into counselling I was struggling with feelings of being a 'non-person', powerless and in despair about ever changing my own life. I could not understand why anyone would get bothered about the possible extinction of rhinoceroses in Central Africa. As I claim my own power, my autonomy and begin to 'own' my life and the repercussions of my existential choices, I begin to feel that those rhinoceroses are *my* rhinoceroses since they represent my response-able connection to my world.'

The Place of the Gestalt Approach in the Field of Counselling

Gestalt values and practice are very compatible with other 'third force' or humanistic/existential approaches such as transactional analysis or psychosynthesis. Many such training programmes integrate Gestalt into their practice and regularly learn from distinguished Gestalt trainers who are either visiting or permanently on their staff.

Carl Rogers, the founder of person-centred counselling approaches, whose work inspires many counselling programmes in Britain, was a very different man from Fritz Perls, but they shared a common faith in the basic drive of human beings towards health, responsibility and self-actualisation.

In some forms of brief psychotherapy primarily based on psychoanalytic tenets such as that of Davanloo, techniques which appear to be directly derived from Gestalt have also been successfully incorporated (Conduit, 1987). But the use of Gestalt techniques grafted onto other ideologies or approaches must be distinguished from the true Gestalt approach where there will be a congruence between the value assumptions, theory, practice and lived experience.

> A Gestalt therapist does not use techniques; he applies *himself in* and *to* a situation with whatever professional skill and life experience he has accumulated and integrated. There are as many styles as there are therapists and clients who discover themselves and each other and together invent their relationship. (Perls, quoted in Smith, 1977: 223)

Gestalt brings to any counselling process a focus on immediacy, relationship and experimentation. It supports and values creativity and spontaneity as well as intelligence in the therapeutic encounter. The Gestalt approach also, along with the other humanistic approaches, contributes a basic faith in, and commitment to, the self-regenerating and self-healing forces of the human being. It is compatible with any other approach which emphasises the unique individuality and responsibility of each human being as he or she freely creates a future in the present moment.

Occasionally Gestaltists sink to claiming or counter-claiming that they are 'more purely Gestalt' than another. In this regard I agree with Yontef (1980: 1).

Three principles define Gestalt therapy. Any therapy regulated by these is indistinguishable from Gestalt therapy, regardless of label, technique or style of the therapist; no therapy violating any of these three is Gestalt therapy. And, any of the three properly and fully understood encompasses the other two:

Principle One: Gestalt therapy is phenomenological; its *only* goal is awareness and its methodology is the methodology of awareness.

Principle Two: Gestalt therapy is based wholly on dialogic existentialism, i.e., the I–You contact/withdrawal process.

Principle Three: Gestalt therapy's conceptual foundation or world view is Gestalt, i.e., based on holism and field theory.

3

THE HEALTHY CYCLE AND ITS APPLICATION TO THE COUNSELLING PROCESS

The Zen master asks: 'Everybody has a place of birth.' (Origin or beginning). 'Where is your place of birth?' The adept answers: 'Early this morning I ate white rice gruel. Now I'm hungry again.'

(Watts, 1962/1974: 125)

The Healthy Cycle of Gestalt Formation and Destruction

As we have seen, Gestalt is not only concerned with pathology; its goal is the re-establishment of the healthiest levels of growth, pleasure and contribution. The healthy uninterrupted flow of experience (emergence of a need to its satisfaction) is the natural state of a healthy animal or a spontaneous natural young child. It is a natural expression of life energy and the drive for actualisation of the self. As the Zen mondo above suggests, a need arises, is satisfied and arises again. A dominant figure emerges from a background, claims attention and fades into the background again as a new compelling figure emerges. This is the cyclic pulsating nature of human experience. Although it may be temporarily inhibited (for example, the freeze response), in service of survival, it will reassert itself as soon as the danger is over. Such an 'instinct cycle' (Perls, 1969a: 69) is a central paradigm in Gestalt theory and practice. Perls conceptualised this instinct cycle as the activity of the *self* as a temporal process evolving in time through the stages of fore-contact, contacting, final contact and post-contact. 'The present is a passage out of the past toward the future, and these are the stages of an act of self as it contacts the actuality' (Perls et al., 1951/1969: 374).

Organismic Flow

The word 'organism' is used in Gestalt in a similar way to the word 'object' in 'object-relations'. The term 'organism' is chosen because it denotes subjectivity, liveliness and biological roots. 'The Organism is a totality of the essential aspects, parts, or organs functioning as a complete unit in persons' (Van De Riet et al., 1980/1985: 36). The Gestalt concept of the organismic flow is represented by the healthy flow of alternating Gestalt formation and destruction which can be likened to the natural breathing pattern of alternating inhalation and exhalation. Every form of life appears as a Gestalt with a specific development in time as well as in space. The rhythm of plants growing, blossoming and seeding is timebound. Indeed according to Von Franz (1978: 32) the meaning of time is that, in it, shapes of growth can unfold in a clear sequence. This book applies this principle to the sequences in counselling. Personal needs likewise arise and are satisfied in such a cyclical or wave-like pattern. This cycle of Gestalt formation and destruction is variously referred to as the awareness cycle, the instinct cycle, the contact-withdrawal cycle or the cycle of experience. The same therapists may teach it differently for different purposes on different days. Different Gestaltists certainly have different opinions about how and where to indicate points of interest along it. It is perhaps most important to use the general idea as a tool from which to develop one's own understanding and integration of different models to facilitate the understanding of healthy and dysfunctional behaviour (Hall, 1977; Melnick and Nevis, 1986; Zinker, 1978). The process could equally well be represented in a wave-like diagram to indicate its rhythmic pulsating quality. Here the cycle is chosen to emphasise systemic circularity, interrelatedness and wholeness. The Gestalt destruction and formation cycle is also chosen with intention to echo the archetypal intuition of a cyclical time in many traditions where the cosmic rhythm consists of periodic destruction and re-creation of the world (Kahn, 1981). Modern physics has revealed that every subatomic particle not only performs an energy dance but also *is* an energy dance, a pulsating process of creation and destruction (Capra, 1976/1978). The seven-stage model presented here (Figure 3.1) is a development based on an integration of Zinker and the original Goodman outline (Perls et al., 1951/1969). It has been found useful in the training of Gestalt counsellors and psychotherapists, as long as they are also encouraged to compare it with other formulations and to develop their own unique perspectives to guide them in their practice.

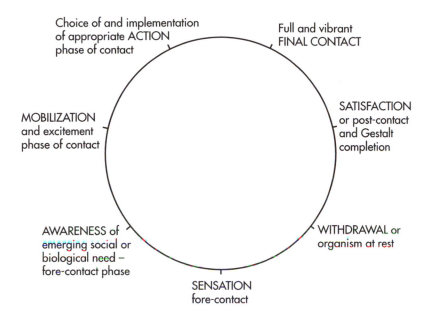

Figure 3.1   *The cycle of Gestalt formation and destruction*

A person is sitting in the garden luxuriating in the spring sunshine after a long winter. His attention is held by bird song, daffodils and playful puppies tugging at a bone. These sights and sounds form the foreground or figure of his field of awareness. Gradually, as it becomes warmer, he loosens his shirt collar. This is not yet a fully formed figure because he is still paying attention to the sights and sounds of the garden. Then as the heat increases a new figure emerges, which is his need to cool off. What was foreground (figure), becomes background. The puppies are no longer occupying his attention; he is now concerned with maintaining his body temperature at a comfortable level. He can do this by moving into the shade, taking off his shirt or going into the coolness of the house. By choosing and implementing appropriate action in relation to his need, he makes way for another need to emerge. In this way there is a constant process where one organismic need follows another through to satisfaction or Gestalt completion.

In psychology, as in physics or astronomy, larger or macroscopic cycles mirror smaller or microscopic cycles. For example, the atom bears a structural resemblance to the solar system. Larger units of experience mirror smaller units. The impatient sigh which lasts a moment can mirror a life lived in frustrated impatience. In this holographic way the whole is represented in each of the parts and the parts each contain a holographic representation of the whole. The Gestalt experience cycle in microcosm (such as in the wave-like pattern of breathing in and breathing out) is a natural process. Depending on what task is at hand, be it running or relaxation, the healthy organism will regulate its breathing to maximum efficiency.

The larger macroscopic cycles, for example the sequences of adult developmental stages, may take a lifetime. Larger or smaller cycles can be managed creatively and satisfactorily if the natural processes are allowed to reach their organismic conclusions.

This simple but also subtle paradigm represents healthy organismic functioning. Any disturbance in this cycle represents 'dis-ease' and will be more fully discussed in the next chapter. This chapter concentrates on the healthy cycle as it relates to the counselling process. If there are no interruptions to the flow, the cycle proceeds in a rhythmic and fulfilling way to meet the changing needs of the person. So, every new emerging need becomes a clear figure until it has been attended to, after which it fades into the background again. This is the phenomenon of 'organismic self-regulation' – that is the way in which people regulate their normal functions such as breathing, eating, sexual activity and elimination, in the course of healthy living. The cycles or wave-like pulsations may range from a very short duration, or span a lengthy period of time (seasonal changes).

Optional Starting Points

The cycle is represented here for the sake of discussion from a particular starting point, i.e. the withdrawal or resting stage. All human cycles do not necessarily originate from one particular point. The model of the instinct cycle is merely a conceptual tool to underline the unified nature of experience. It is not meant to indicate causes. Gestalt is more about 'how', than about 'why'. Elsewhere discussions of the cycle will start from the sensation phase.

A wife nags, her husband withdraws so she nags some more. Or the husband withdraws, his wife nags, so he withdraws some more. Is it the wife's nagging that 'causes' the husband's withdrawal, or the husband's

withdrawal that 'causes' the wife's nagging? From a phenomenological perspective of their relationship in the here-and-now, both are equally
responsible for the process which maintains the undesirable situation and
it is 'the fault' of neither. Arbitrary assignation of 'causes' is antithetical to
the Gestalt approach. Gestaltists would frequently view the couple and
their relational field as a unified whole where each is simultaneously both
causal and reactive to the other's behaviour in their *system*.

Stages of the Cycle

Theoretically and experientially this cycle can be viewed from any chosen
angle. Any point of attention represents but a punctuation point in an
ongoing living system, not an invariable starting block. Figure 3.1 represents one view among many of differentially different phases in this cycle.
The different stages of the cycle are meant to draw attention to sequentially
differing *points of focus* in the process of Gestalt formation and destruction. Because of the static nature of the written word it may appear that
there are discrete dividing lines between one phase and another. This is not
so; such a misconception would be an artefact of attempting to capture the
essence of a breaking ocean wave in a technical drawing or a mathematical
formula. In a true Gestalt sense, whenever one phase is in ascendance, the
others are background. It would be a violation to divide human rhythms
into discrete confined stages. At all times the reader would do well to
remember that these shade into each other, that they develop and subdi-
vide and merge like the rest of nature's timetables; difficult to forecast
exactly correctly, but better than not having any idea of when seedlings can
be planted out without danger of frost.

Withdrawal

The first phase of the cyclical sequence to be discussed here is that of *withdrawal or rest*. In this resting phase the person can be balanced or centred
between Gestalt formation and destruction. There is no clear figure and
the organism is in a state of homeostasis or perfect balance – it's neither too
hot nor too cold; the person is neither in a state of sexual excitation nor in
a state of sexual deprivation; neither anxious nor excited. This is the calm
resting phase that follows on from satisfactory completion of a Gestalt, for
example post-orgasmic quiescence. It is a period when there is no strong
foreground figure impinging on our awareness. 'This state is pregnant with

the limitless range of potential developments for the fully alive person. 'What interesting thing might happen next' is the quiet, confident, open, poised question' (Hall, 1977: 53).

Sensation

The organism (or person) cannot remain at rest for an indefinite period. New organismic deficits or surpluses must arise in the living person. Either internal or external disturbances in the form of a need which is striving for gratification *or* a demand made upon us will impinge upon the homeostatic balance of organism and environment.

Either gradually or suddenly a figure will emerge from this undifferentiated 'ground' and become 'figure' for us. For example, the desire for a cup of tea. Perls et al. (1951/1969) distinguish the following four classes of such sensory or proprioceptive excitation:

1   Periodic urges and appetites which strive for contact with the environment, for example hunger and affection.
2   A periodic pain, a tension headache for example, where the contact or figure relates more inwardly to the body.
3   Stimulations either developing as appetites, emotions or pains which are precipitated by events in the environment such as a rejecting telephone call or a loving hug from a friend.
4   Physiological readjustments which occur in response to changes in the environment which might be changes in temperature, level of stimulation, noise, an earthquake!

Perls, Hefferline and Goodman identify these as *'fore-contacts'* which herald the start of the figure/background formation process. It could be said to refer to the stage where raw sensory proprioceptive information begins to register but before these possibilities come fully into meaningful awareness.

Awareness

We may gradually or suddenly become aware of any of these events impinging sensorily or proprioceptively on our free-floating consciousness. The novel figure that emerges becomes the focal point of interest in our experience of the moment. The stronger and more urgent this figure – for example, a fire alarm – the clearer and more immediate our response is likely to be. The desire to have a glass of water during a lecture may take a longer time to become a figure strong enough to motivate one to attend to one's thirst (organismic imbalance).

'Awareness is a form of experiencing. It is the process of being in a vigilant contact with the most important event in the individual/environment field, with full sensorimotor, emotional, cognitive, and energetic support' (Yontef, 1979b: 29). It is a meaning-making function which creates fresh Gestalten – new insight into the obvious unity of disparate pieces of self-knowledge, or consciousness – as if for the first time, of the fruity perfumed golden spray of breaking a piece of orange skin.

When the situation calls for an awareness of the past or anticipation of the future, effective awareness takes this into account (Simkin and Yontef, 1984: 290). For example, a man in his fifties who has made an enormous success of his career, comes for counselling. He has become aware of a gradual dissatisfaction with the emotional emptiness of his relationships with family and friends. Before he sought worldly success as figure or dominant need; now the quality of his relationships has become increasingly important. His awareness of this new need pushes for attention, towards the future, driving his previous ambitions into the background.

Mobilisation

Awareness of a need is usually followed by excitement and *mobilisation* of self and resources. At this state of emotional and/or physiological arousal the object-figure or need becomes sharper and clearer, generating energy and images of possibilities for satisfaction. The healthy person in this phase is breathing deeply and freely, the motor system is activated for movement and the senses are open to maximum information from the surroundings.

For example, a young adult comes for career counselling. Anne is intelligent and talented in many directions. She is excited at the prospect of an academic career but she wants counselling to enable her to make the best choices from the many exciting options. In the counselling process it would be important to investigate what field of study is most likely to be sustained under prolonged stress or over long periods of time, such as a three-year or a five-year course of study. This phase in the healthy cycle is likened to the excitement and mobilisation phase of *contact* as described by Perls et al. (1951/1969).

Action

Another punctuation point in the process of contact (or figure formation) as a single whole can be identified as the '*contacting*' phase of choosing and implementing appropriate *action* (Perls et al., 1951/1969). This includes the organisation of perceptual, behavioural and emotional activity. The client chooses and rejects possibilities. The person actively reaches out towards possibilities, seeking to overcome obstacles and experimenting with different forms of appropriate action. Behaviours are relevant to the optimal fulfilment of needs in the here-and-now reality. An unemployed thirty-year-old man makes numerous applications for jobs, regularly investigates job-centre opportunities and engages in voluntary work to keep himself alert and interested at the same time as maintaining continuity in his employment-experience by keeping up with the latest methods.

Final Contact

Choosing and implementing the appropriate action based on energetic consideration of the possibilities, both in reality and in imagination, is naturally followed by full and vibrant contact or what Goodman (Perls et al., 1951/1969: 403) called 'final contact'.

Our sensory and motor functions (seeing, hearing, feeling, moving, touching) are potentially the functions through which contact is made. It is important to remember that just as the whole is more than merely a sum of its parts, contact is more than the sum of all the possible functions that may go into it. Seeing and hearing are no guarantee of good contact, it is rather *how* one sees or hears that determines good contact. Contact can be made with objects or aspects of nature as well as with animals or people, with memories, images, aspects of oneself. It is the quality of the contact which makes the difference between the sun going down and the rich, vivid and full experiencing of a piercingly multi-flamed sunset.

Contact takes place at the *boundary of the self and the environment*, and is our profoundest intercourse with our world. It is the quintessential distillation of focused attention becoming for a time inseparable from the focus of attention. It is the moment of delicious climactic merging during lovemaking, the shivers down the spine during a stirring piece of music; it is the total absorption when the final pieces of a creative problem start clicking together. It also applies to yawning, putting out the cat and arguing. The quality of contact determines whether life 'passes by' or whether it is lived and experienced to the full. After many years of stoic resignation following a bereavement, a dam of tears eventually breaks in a client. He gasps through his sobs, 'I'm hurting, I'm crying and I feel whole!'

This is Gestalt – not changing what is or wishing it different, but re-establishing the natural expressiveness, mobility and vividness of moment-by-moment experiences, whether these be in phases of explosion or quietude.

> Furthermore, contact extends into interaction with inanimate as well as animate objects; to see a tree or a sunset or to hear a waterfall or a cave's silence is contact. Contact can also be made with memories and images, experiencing them sharply and fully . . . contact is a dynamic relationship occurring only at the boundaries of two compellingly attractive but clearly differentiated figures of interest. The differentiation can distinguish between one organism and another, or an organism and some novel inanimate object in its environment, or an organism and some novel quality of itself. (Polster and Polster, 1974: 102–8)

Good *contact* is a core idea in Gestalt. Perceptually, it is equivalent to focusing clearly and vividly on the most important aspect of a personal situation without extraneous or background stimuli distorting the fullness of attention or the quality of the interaction. An auditory example concerns the way in which one can often clearly hear the conversation of one's partner in a crowded party amidst the almost deafening sounds of several other loud conversations and raucous music in one's immediate vicinity. A visual example is the way in which the rest of thronging humanity blurs into the background as the figure of a loved one emerges from the mass at an airport. Full experiencing of a glass of wine or a friendship is analogous with these examples. The enjoyment of both can be more or less complete to the extent that extraneous and irrelevant influences are screened out or relegated to the background. For a few moments, or even more, the clear vivid figure is the only Gestalt in existence, imbuing the here-and-now with a richness and clarity which is exquisitely spontaneous, uniting perception, movement and emotion in unitary action, whether it be full-bodied expression of grief or a sexual climax.

This full and final contact marks the closure of a particular Gestalt. Momentarily the person is completely engaged in the figure she has created, or discovered. Healthy contact is characterised by this whole-hearted and full-bodied engagement with that which is most significant for the person at a given moment. It is a basic need of human beings to be in such contact with other people (as well as to be separate from them). Contact is the source of our richest joy and our most intensely painful moments. 'Contact is implicitly incompatible with remaining the same. Through contact, though, one does not have to *try* to change; change simply occurs' (Polster and Polster, 1974: 101). True contact, paradoxically, opens the gateways to change. The cycle moves on.

Satisfaction

The next identifiable phase is that which Perls et al. (1951/1969) called *post-contact*. It refers essentially to satisfaction and Gestalt completion. This is the phase where the person experiences deep organismic satisfaction, and can be compared to the 'afterglow' following full and complete experiences of intimacy or creative expression. An image that captures this time is that of a mother with a naked new baby nestling at her body which moments before had been part of her. This is the quiet after the storm, the precious moments before separation or withdrawal begins. This is a process of digestion and assimilation, when the person can spit out what is not acceptable or nourishing – necessary follow-up to the activities of destructuring and absorption.

This post-contact or satisfaction phase is frequently omitted from theoretical discussions of the cycle. This may be a reflection of the lack of importance sometimes accorded to the closing phases of human experiences. However, we know that saying goodbye only becomes truly meaningful when we fully appreciate what we are leaving behind. It is common for people to worry about events for long periods before they happen; it is less usual for people to celebrate events for long sustained periods after they have happened. Perhaps in a masculine culture the early active, thrusting parts of the cycle are over-valued compared to the later more archetypically female phases. Yet this period of gradual assimilation, of 'coming down', of savouring experiences as they are receding from focus and fading into the background can be the source of deep pleasure or profound learning.

> The experience of transition, a simple movement through time, easily eludes people as they cope with complex daily requirements. Yet since nothing stays still, except as we may imagine it, we all live at the transition point between now and next. It is through this movement that people stay fresh and through it that the stories of our lives grow. The therapist, as well as the novelist, attends

to the recognition and enhancement of this inevitable movement, even when his patient may not yet see it. (Polster, 1987: 67)

Withdrawal

The phase of post-contact is followed again by *withdrawal* into the 'fertile void' from whence sensations heralding a new need can emerge again. Then the cycle of self-regulation has recommenced with the person experiencing the emptiness of 'the void' – the neutral transition zone which follows withdrawal and precedes sensation. The external cycle is not different from the internal one, and the principles apply as much to more subtle functions such as the need for physical contact or peer esteem or artistic self-expression as to the biological needs for food, oxygen and defecation.

The Stages of the Counselling Process Related to the Healthy Cycle

Sensation

People commonly become aware of their desire for counselling when there is some internal or external disturbance to the homeostasis of their lives. The hormonal imbalances of adolescence often coincide with emotional storms which bring them and their families to counsellors. Changes in the socioeconomic system (organism-environment field) may also upset the status quo. The miners' strike in Britain precipitated many families into a re-evaluation of their roles, their beliefs and their political allegiances.

Often the first stirrings of discontent are experienced as physical sensation – a recurrent tightness in the chest, a lingering cold, an unforgiving headache or increasingly disturbed breathing.

Frances, a faded fifty-year-old mother, comes for counselling. She dutifully followed the precepts of her childhood upbringing and identified with the gender stereotypes of the 1950s. Her third child has recently left home for university and she is experiencing feelings of loss and grief as she needs to re-evaluate the meaning of her life after 'her nest has emptied'. Up to this point in her history she has never felt the need for counselling but she is currently bewildered and perplexed by the social, physiological and intellectual changes in her life. Whereas her husband appears less interested in sex, and wishes to spend more time in front of the television, she finds herself more interested in sex than she had been for many years.

Awareness

This new awareness of herself and her emotional needs acts as a spur to seek counselling. Heightened awareness of her need to talk to someone about these changes in her life makes her more observant of magazine articles discussing personal problems. She finds herself listening to radio phone-ins. She discovers that several of her friends have in the past sought counselling and she enquires about their experiences.

Mobilisation

At the point of mobilisation the tension related to her emerging need becomes energised. Her excitement is manifested in changes in her autonomic nervous system as she experiences a general sense of arousal. She mobilises the relevant resources in herself and in her environment, including an estimate of what counselling might cost. She is willing to open herself emotionally and intellectually to the counselling process. Frances now telephones for an appointment to the counsellor who was recommended by her most trusted friend. A few days later she is to meet her counsellor for the first time. As she travels to his consulting room she experiences an increase in her heart rate, rapid breathing and the excitement of being faced with a novel situation. She recognises that this feeling has some similarities with anxiety, but knows that there is no real danger involved in this exploratory contact. So she looks forward to a rewarding meeting, trusting that even if it is not always a pleasant process, she is bound to learn from the encounter.

Action

This is the stage where Frances goes into action. She chooses and implements appropriate action by organising her perceptual, emotional and behavioural activities with the goal of meeting her primary emergent need. This need she earlier identified as the desire to actualise herself and her potentialities beyond the roles prescribed for her by society. In the first phases of the counselling relationship, most of her emotional and mental energy is concerned with forming a working alliance with her counsellor. She asks him questions about his training, supervision and his position on confidentiality. Using her own judgement and intuition about him as a person, she decides that he is trustworthy and is willing to disclose more and more of herself – even those parts which thus far she has avoided. She can express her anger at the restrictions imposed upon her by an education system, and at male teachers who never seriously considered her scientific potentials.

In the counselling relationship she is enabled to experiment and explore her needs; and she is supported in separating herself from expectations of the mother-and-wife role imposed upon her by society and family. She begins to develop a sense of herself as a separate person with heightened sensory awareness and a finely tuned sensitivity to her own physiological and psychological processes. She engages in experiments and structures which help her to consider the messages and self-definitions which she had metaphorically 'swallowed' as a young girl and she begins to review these, deciding which she would like to keep, which to spit out and which to chew, savour and digest.

She experiments with different options for fulfilment in her life such as starting her own business in catering, having an affair, going to university to study as a chemical engineer. She keeps a dream diary, takes up pottery as an expressive medium and seeks out role models of women who change their careers in mid-life.

Final Contact

Contact in the counselling process involves full and complete awareness of as many aspects of the problematical situation as possible. The 'stuck point' or 'impasse' has become the total figure which must be resolved before the person can comfortably resume the developmental journey. Often this coincides with the person re-owning his or her full range of emotional responses – rage, fear, sadness and joy.

Getting in touch with and expressing the accumulated hurts and disappointments of her life in the context of an accepting and enabling relationship, empowers Frances to bring all her intellectual, behavioural and psychological resources to bear on her problem.

During this phase, Frances resolves her conflict between what she wants to do, which is to actualise all her latent potential and what she used to believe she 'should' do, which is to settle comfortably into middle-aged spread and knitting jumpers for her grandchildren.

This period of true contact is the climax of the counselling process, often experienced as a 'metanoia' (a turning about) (Burchfield, 1976: 911). After this the client cannot conceive of returning to her earlier way of being. The significant components in her social system are also affected by her changes. Her husband and children have moved beyond their initial scepticism and insecurities and are valuing and reinforcing Frances's growing competence and confidence in her newly found self. Her husband is intrigued and excited by her rediscovered sensuality and willingness to take risks in sexual experimentation. Her daughters mourn the loss of 'safe and secure old mum', but also take pride when they attend her graduation ceremony at the university.

Satisfaction

The satisfaction phase marks the enjoyment and integration stage of counselling. No longer are the sessions fraught with conflicting feelings and ambivalent emotions, but there is a clear sense of a developmental task well accomplished. Frances is no longer frustrated and she has overcome some of her initial fears about testing her intelligence and her social skills on campus. She sometimes looks back on her earlier life envying the simplicity of that time when she was less aware of her responsibility to herself. However, the rewards and richness of her full commitment to her path of self-development and self-actualisation seem eminently preferable. The counselling relationship becomes less and less important and the consulting room becomes more a place where she shares the fruits of her awareness and celebrates her successes.

Withdrawal

In the last stages of the healthy cycle of counselling, the client prepares for separation from the counselling relationship. He or she has learnt many of the skills and techniques for enhanced self-awareness and more efficient problem-solving from the counsellor, and can now use these without guidance.

Frances bids the counsellor a fond farewell. She is sad that this contact that has been so nourishing and important for her is now terminating. Yet she is excited and pleased at the prospect of continuing her growth without his assistance. She has built up for herself other supportive structures such as a professional women's networking group which she attends on a regular basis. Her husband has become her friend as well as mate. Her new life, with all its richness and challenge, has become figure. Her experience with counselling fades into the background.

Microscopic Cycles within Macroscopic Cycles

The healthy cycle in the counselling process has been described. It may take a few weeks or several years. But since the nature of this cycle appears to be constant across situations and time, it also will be manifest in a single session. In most counselling sessions clients will move from awareness of their most pressing need to mobilisation of energy to deal with it, to organising at perceptual, emotional and physiological levels for full and complete expression or encounter. In a functional cycle this completion is followed by satisfaction and enjoyment making place for the next important issue to emerge.

   In this chapter an ideal sequence in the counselling process has been described where client and counsellor moved, almost without hiccup, through an orderly progression of Gestalt formation and completion. Of course, it is rarely this easy in real life. It is more likely that there will be many false starts, uneven progressions, regressions and arhythmic plateaux. The next chapter will address some of the many varied ways in which the smooth and harmonious function of this cycle can be disturbed.

4

DYSFUNCTIONS AND DISTURBANCES IN THE CYCLE

MONK: Do you ever make an effort to get disciplined in the truth?
MASTER: Yes I do. When I am hungry, I eat; when I am tired, I sleep.
MONK : This is what everybody does.
MASTER : No.
MONK : Why not?
MASTER : Because when they eat, they do not eat; they are thinking of various other things, thereby allowing themselves to be disturbed.

(Suzuki, 1949)

An holistic perspective on the origins, mechanisms and phases of 'dis-ease' will be followed by a more detailed discussion of particular components of the process. In the true spirit of Gestalt, please bear in mind that the living whole is always more than the sum of its analysed parts. Any part of this discussion is but a temporary cross-section of an ongoing and evolving process.

The Concept of 'Dis-ease'

One of the fundamental concepts of Gestalt theory is that the person is basically healthy and is striving for balance, health and growth. Therefore, any approach which presumes the human being to be essentially flawed is incompatible with the Gestalt approach. Perls drew attention to the fact that plants and animals do not prevent their own growth – only humans do. Even though he used the word 'neurosis', he wrote that actually 'it should be called *growth disorder*' (1969b: 28).

For the Gestaltist the guiding vision is the healthy, self-regulating essence of the person. The healing task is to facilitate the removal of impediments, hindrances and obstacles to the self-actualisation process. For most people disease has connotations of an illness about which medical and psychological experts are consulted. Gestaltists often prefer to use the term 'dis-ease' to describe a condition in which the person is not fully functioning, to emphasise the process of not-being-at-ease or not-being-in-harmony. 'As action, contact, choice and authenticity characterize health in gestalt therapy, so stasis, resistance, rigidity and control, often with anxiety, characterize the state called 'dis-ease" (Van de Riet et al., 1980/1985: 60). When people are 'dis-eased' they are not experiencing themselves as whole persons in good psychological and physiological relationship with their environment. They are not effectively going through the awareness cycle with ease, grace and efficiency.

At a microscopic level a gross psychophysiological holding-in pattern (such as not breathing out completely by keeping the chest inflated) disturbs the natural flow of the breathing. This impedes the person's ability to use breath effectively to support chosen goals. In the same way the person's inability to let go of old habits and outdated identities on a psychological level can disturb the person's availability for new experiences. Ill-health occurs when the process of Gestalt formation–destruction–reformation has been disturbed. Some Gestaltists conceive of the cycle as being disturbed *between* each of the different phases, for example between sensation and awareness, awareness and mobilisation and so on (Zinker, 1978). The approach used in this book is built on Perls et al. (1951/1969) who conceptualised most of the interruptions at or *during* the corresponding phases of the instinct cycle. (Different approaches can be fruitful since interruptions can be conceptualised as occurring between stages, during them or around them. Of course, since these are but concepts reaching towards representing human experience any view is partial; no approach is 'true'.) The Gestalt awareness cycle itself is always healthy, based as it is on the cycle of experience or the probable sequences of natural need fulfilment of the person. To the extent that the original organismic need is denied or displaced, there can be no true satisfaction, the cycle will be essentially off-target, and the person will be in a state of dis-ease.

'Unfinished Business' and the Fixed Gestalt

Unfinished Business

The idea of 'unfinished business' is a core notion in the Gestalt approach to explain how energy becomes blocked or 'interrupted'. It refers to the fact that the only constant flow is the forming of 'Gestalten' – wholes, completenesses, or organic units. Every urge or need which arises drives us to do something to complete the organismic cycle. When we have done this its purpose is fulfilled. An emergent need may be related to the here-and-now reality such as going to the toilet; or it might be related to unfinished business from the past seeking completion in the present, such as seeking approval from a parent.

> This situation is now closed and the next unfinished situation can take its place, which means that our life is basically practically nothing but an infinite number of unfinished situations – incomplete gestalts. No sooner have we finished one situation than another comes up. (Perls, 1969b: 15)

When people do not move easily and spontaneously around the awareness cycle to get their needs met, the event is unfinished. Some episode of childhood history, some important early need, was left unsatisfied and the person did not complete the cycle in a way that was right for him or her biologically or psychologically. For example, a child not being allowed to grieve (or cry) for the death of a beloved pet may lead the grown-up person to withhold affection from new attachments since the original grief was not allowed its full expression in a way that was healthful/harmonious for animals and human beings.

Similarly, experiences of pain, resentment or anger towards other people need to be resolved by assertive action (for which breathing in is a metaphor) or acceptance of letting go (for which breathing out is a metaphor). Without such resolution the experience is incomplete or not finished, and available energy and psychological resources are held in (repressed) around the 'unfinished situation'. Physiologically, the equivalent of psychologically incomplete Gestalten manifests when people develop character/body armouring which keeps their chests collapsed in a position of resignation, or when they habitually hold back some of their breath in an inflated 'barrel-chested' position of threatened aggressiveness. The unfinished business may be unsatisfactory past relationships, for example, unexpressed protest against parental cruelty; or it may be regret for not fulfilling certain potentials of the self.

The psychological energy of the person becomes bound or repressed out of awareness. This repression then drains away resources available for experiencing life in its richness in the here-and-now with full psychological and physiological responsiveness. Rivalrous feelings towards a sibling which were not allowed connected expression ('Of course you love your baby brother') may manifest in adulthood as a chronic back pain behind the right shoulder. This displaces the original need to protest by anchoring it in the back muscles. In this way the need is alienated from the original target, neither released nor fully bearable. Physically and psychologically the unfinished situation continues to 'press for closure' since the original situation is not satisfactorily completed and neither can the person fully enjoy the potential satisfactions of the present moment in current relationships which may not be as rivalrous as the earlier one. Of course adult pathology does not always result from a single such event, but develops from a whole matrix of variables including the person's present life situation.

The Urge to Complete

Unfinished business represents an incomplete Gestalt. However, the completion of wholes is such a rudimentary fact of human nature that human beings *do* complete them even if in a warped, distorted or pathological way. In the healthy Gestalt awareness cycle, when the baby experiences a need such as hunger, he mobilises his energies and acts by crying loudly for a caretaker to feed him. When this appropriate action is met by full and good contact with the environment (the feeding by the caretaker) the need is met and the hunger is satisfied. The baby experiences satisfaction as is evident from the relaxation of his mouth round the nipple and the contented expression on his face. Then, naturally a new need emerges. This may be a need for sleep, for cuddles or for stimulation. Whatever it is, if the new need is followed through on the awareness cycle and satisfactorily completed, another new need will emerge.

In this way the organismic cycle repeats itself over and over again in the healthy person as each new need is appropriately met. The basic needs being met can be infinitely diverse, ranging from the complex need to finish a symphonic composition once in a lifetime to the simple regularity of hygiene or elimination. In a less than optimal situation the infant cries from hunger and the caretakers do not respond appropriately. Healthy infants will tend to escalate their demands at this point, screaming more loudly and more stridently until some caretaker responds. This is the way in which the baby takes responsibility for getting his needs met, i.e. by letting the world know about them. In the unfortunate event that the care-taker(s) still do not appropriately meet the hunger needs of the little person, 'shut-down' occurs. This is the point at which the infant 'gives up' (Bowlby, 1953) and the Gestalt is 'fixed' in a pathological manner.

At this point of suppression the strong and primitive feelings of the infant are suppressed in favour of his survival. This goes along with phys-iological changes which may manifest in holding patterns in the body, for example a tightly clenched jaw. Because of the natural drive for completion counsellors also discover that infants and children make some kind of cog-nitive closure to their early trauma or chronic deprivation. As children, many people found or made explanations of why their primary needs for understanding or nurturance were not met. Often these explanations are incorrect, based as they are on pre-operational levels of thinking which are pre-logical, often symbolic and frequently imbued with magical charac-teristics. This was how at best, at that time, the organism could reach completion so as to move on to the next emerging need.

A baby may experience a basic sense of worthlessness because his mother made it clear that she disliked handling his body and dealing with his natural functions. In a very primitive pre-logical sense the infant may seek a reason for this. He may feel that it is due to something being very wrong with him. He may later overhear that he nearly caused his mother's death in childbirth. This builds on the infantile sense of wrongness or badness and becomes incorporated in the person's self-image in the future. This combination of affective, cognitive and physiological closure becomes a fixed Gestalt – a repetitive and predictable behaviour pattern in relation to the world and other people. Each time the person attempts to meet the original need but fails over and over again, since it is based on the original organismic experience of failure. Thus compulsion to repeat is understood to stem from a failure to complete.

Dysfunctions in the Flow of the Cycle

According to Gestalt theory there are several psychological mechanisms by means of which we maintain in the present unfinished situations from the past, deprive ourselves of the fulfilment of our needs and impede good contact with ourselves, others and the environment. These are sometimes referred to as *boundary disturbances* since they can be seen as fixations which interfere with healthy functioning of the creative self at the organism/environment boundary. In Gestalt these are also viewed as self-regulating acts, and include defensive functions. It is vital to emphasise a process orientation based on the dynamic interaction of organism and environment since this enhances the possibility of change. Any or all of the boundary disturbances discussed here may interfere specifically at the final contact phase of the awareness cycle. However all of them may permeate any or all of the stages of the whole *process*.

Perls (Perls et al., 1951/1969) specifically focused on confluence, introjection, projection and retroflection as the most prevalent means of interrupting contact; Goodman (Perls et al., 1951/1969) also used egotism and the Polsters (Polster and Polster, 1974) added deflection. Desensitisation (Perls 1969b) is also occasionally used. Other authors have experimented with combinations of these, but for the purposes of this introductory book these seven major mechanisms will be discussed.

It is important to note that most of the classic Gestalt theorists such as Perls (1969b), Polster and Polster (1974), as well as Melnick and Nevis (1986), acknowledge occasions in adult life where autonomously chosen and intentional use of any of the interruptions to contact may be a healthy option and in service of the organism. This needs to be taken into consideration as I discuss these interruptions, which may be chronically or acutely pathological at different times for different individuals.

According to Perls et al. (1951/1969), these mechanisms are only neurotic when they are used chronically and inappropriately. All of them are useful and healthy when authentically chosen and used temporarily in particular circumstances by choice, not compulsion. However, they are unhealthy when they are fixated on impossible or non-existent objects, when they involve an impoverishment of awareness and when they prevent meaningful integration of needs and experiences.

Each neurotic mechanism interlocks with the others and they are functionally interrelated. For example, introjection and confluence are necessary for projection or retroflection to occur. Consideration of these interruptions should not be in terms of the classification of neurotic people, but a method of investigating the structure of a single neurotic behaviour.

This is obvious on the face of it, for every neurotic mechanism is a fixation and every mechanism contains a confluence, something unaware. Likewise every behaviour is resigned to some false-identification, disowns an emotion, turns aggression against the self, and is conceited! What the scheme means to show is the *order* in which, against the background of a threatened repression, the fixation spreads through the entire process of contact, and the unawareness comes to meet it from the other direction. (Perls et al., 1951/1969: 458)

Particular boundary disturbances may tend to be more prominent at different phases of the cycle of Gestalt formation and destruction. The order or sequence in which the neurotic mechanisms may unfold implies that other phases of the cycle will be impeded, handicapped or prevented from fulfilment to the extent that any other phase is incomplete, distorted or damaged.

Dis-ease can therefore be seen as a disturbance in the flow of the Gestalt formation cycle or a dysfunction in any one or more phases of the cycle. What is of importance is where and how these notions are found useful in the therapeutic encounter. Dysfunction in the *sensation* phase (sometimes called 'desensitisation') often occurs when sensations from the body such as pain or discomfort are ignored and information from the environment is also blocked out.

An example of this kind of disturbance may occur when Jocelyn regularly allows herself to get too cold as she works late into the night. Having been abused as a child, she is as an adult estranged from her physical self. The psychophysiological scars of her early injuries prevent her from registering at a very basic level when she is hurt, hungry or tired. She has succeeded in screening out painful stimuli, but she has also isolated herself from all the basic pleasures and joys of life. She comes to counselling on the recommendation of her employers who see her working at all hours like an efficient automaton, but they have become concerned at the long-term consequences for her health. Clients with schizoid personality traits usually show some significant disturbance of sensation by minimising or distorting the impact of internal sensations or external stimuli.

Dysfunction around the *awareness* phase of the Gestalt-formation cycle (later in this chapter this is expanded on under the term 'deflection') occurs when the person is not fully aware of his or her own needs or the demands and invitations of the environment. Neither awareness of information from their own bodies, nor awareness from the outside is given significant meaning. People may disturb the emergence of a new figure at this stage by not paying attention or by deliberately diverting attention from that which is most significant to their well-being or need-fulfilment.

People who have passive aggressive personality traits may prevent stimuli from others making an impact on them by blocking their awareness. For example, Peter is in a 'sulk'. He sits withdrawn, staring out of the window and is frowning. Lucy asks him: 'What's wrong?' In a voice redolent with contempt he says, 'Nothing'. In this way he is 'tuning her out' and minimising any impact she may have on him.

In the next phase of this cycle, that which emphasises *mobilisation*, dysfunction can occur when there is insufficient or excessive mobilisation of energies, or when excitement is blocked or misinterpreted. Clients who are very depressed exemplify a disturbance of this part of the cycle because of their inability to mobilise their energies, such as when they stop eating or caring for themselves. This is frequently in response to toxic introjects, for example an internalised abusive or neglectful parent. Generalised excitement and unspecific mobilisation can be seen in anxiety states. Jenny complains that she feels anxious most of the time in her college classes. Her energies are certainly aroused, potentially available and discharging. However, her state of arousal when she sits perched on the front of her seat in the lecture room, muscles ready to run and hyperventilating in a state of alertness, does not lead to goal-directed action or satisfactory Gestalt completion. Mobilisation needs to be chosen or implemented appropriately to relieve her anxiety or to be freely available for the intellectual nourishment which she also seeks. Jenny imagines that the lecturer and her fellow students should despise her and would consider her boring and worthless. In working with Jenny in counselling it becomes clear that these negative messages in her head have their origin in her childhood when she 'introjected' (or internalised) her parents' destructive attributions. Now these have become her own beliefs about her worthlessness as a person and a friend, and she behaves accordingly in 'unfriendly' and 'boring' ways.

Around the *action* phase of the cycle, dysfunction can occur when action is chosen and implemented but is not appropriate to the fulfilment of the primary organismic need. Frequently the disturbance in this part of the cycle is due to disowning parts of the self and attributing them to others ('projection') as in paranoid disturbances. Projection prevents the person from being fully and completely 'in touch' with the action needed to complete a sensation or an experience. In fact, actions may be repeated over and over again as in the compulsions or the addictions, but these actions are not effective in dealing with the real need. For instance, when Jake is anxious he gets involved in obsessive tidying instead of acknowledging his long-forgotten desire to be understood and taken seriously.

Around the *final contact* phase of the cycle, dysfunction may occur when the action does not fully, energetically and vibrantly connect or discharge appropriately. Instead of acting on the environment and directing the behaviour to an appropriate external target, these people turn their behaviour in upon themselves. This is later explained under 'retroflection'. For example, instead of risking intimacy (and rejection) by seeking loving relationships with other people, Claus daydreams excessively and 'pampers' himself with food, massages and expensive clothes. Rather than express her anger towards her abusive boss, Alvyn turns angrily on herself and berates herself for being the kind of person who is always victimised. She would never speak out against the boss, but she has frequent attacks of laryngitis where she experiences herself 'strangling herself' – much as she would like to do to him in fantasy.

Subtle electrochemical muscular responses of the body (which are prevented from expression by inhibition or good sense) can result in permanent character armouring or even contribute to the more or less serious manifestations of physical disease such as diabetes, arthritis and cancer.

Around the post-contact or *satisfaction* phase of the cycle of awareness, disruption can occur when a person does not savour the fullness and completeness of experience, rushing on prematurely from one experience to another. People who habitually interrupt their experience at this phase do not derive a sense of completion from most of their experiences. They are left in some vague way feeling deprived of the pleasant 'after-taste' that follows a good meal or a challenging confrontation from a friend. One of the ways in which contact is not necessarily fully satisfactory contact is when you are 'aware of being in contact'. That would be like being in love and 'self-consciously' keeping copies of your love poetry. The experience of watching or commenting on yourself or your performance is referred to as 'egotism' in Gestalt or 'spectatoring' in sex therapy, and resembles narcissistic personality patterns. Many women who experience difficulties with having orgasms during intercourse are demonstrating a problem at this stage of the awareness cycle. Satisfaction with contact is more the sense of gravity when standing or walking, not thinking to yourself how aware you are of making good contact with the grass underfoot. It is the full and vibrant experiencing of 'grassness'.

Such dysfunctions at this phase of the awareness cycle result in a lack of spontaneity and an alienation from the physical self and the environment. People who chronically interrupt contact here may seem 'in control' of themselves, but they lack the unself-conscious ease of being 'in tune' with themselves and their environment. Metaphorically they are 'pushing the river' (Stevens, 1970).

After satisfaction follows the stage of complete *withdrawal* or rest which can lead to a state of balance, quiescence and openness. Disruption occurs when the person is reluctant to let go of a previous situation or rushes on to a new figure. In this way he or she can avoid the state of 'being in the void', before some clear figure arises spontaneously from the self or from the environment. This is characteristic of people who have difficulty in letting go. There may be problems in relinquishing a self-image or stage of life such as trauma when moving to a new house. Letting go of past associations and experiences, and the grieving for them, is a necessary part of detaching and opening oneself to the possibilities and potentials of a new attachment. It is what is referred to as the 'neutral zone' in transition theory (Bridges, 1980/1984). 'Workaholics' or professional people who allow themselves to 'burn out' may exemplify chronic disturbances in this part of the cycle. The satisfactions of work have become all-encompassing and their attachment to (or 'confluence' with) the source of satisfaction, has become a blockage to their deriving pleasure from other sources. Reluctance to enter this neutral zone, or avoidance of it, constitutes a disturbance in the harmonious rhythmical pulsation of the Gestalt formation cycle.

Interferences or disturbances at any part of this cycle naturally interfere with the elegant and natural rhythm of need-fulfilment of a person. In this way, confluence may prevent satisfactory development of the sensation phase, desensitisation may prevent full awareness, deflection interferes with mobilisation, introjection may impede effective action, projection prevents good final contact and retroflection diminishes the satisfaction phase and egotism limits effective withdrawal.

Figure 4.1 represents a summary diagram of the cycle of Gestalt formation and destruction with illustrative examples of characteristic boundary disturbances, for our purposes here located at each stage. If the inner part of the circle can represent the self and the part of the field outside the circle can represent the environment, then the line between the two represents the boundary between them. This is the edge of the organism–environment exchange. The seven boundary disturbances discussed here are indicated by smaller arrowed lines with a small circle attached representing intrapsychic material or environmental resources.

In order to facilitate mental digestion of this material a metaphor of

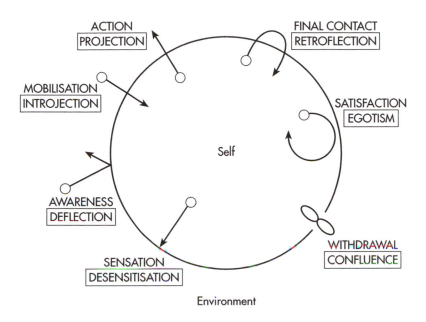

Figure 4.1   *The cycle of Gestalt formation and destruction with diagrammatic examples of boundary disturbances at each stage*

eating-related behaviour may be helpful. So, in desensitisation intrapsychic stimuli are blocked at the boundary from the inside. Desensitisation is like eating with frozen lips and without taste buds. In deflection, stimuli from outside are prevented from penetrating the organism–environment boundary similar to clenching the teeth to prevent anything being ingested. In introjection, external material is incorporated too easily – food is swallowed whole, without chewing or tasting. In projection, intrapsychic material is ejected too easily like spitting or vomiting out what had already been ingested. In retroflection, material which is intended for an external target is turned in on itself. This is metaphorically similar to stroking or biting your own lip. In egotism, intrapsychic material is recycled without reference to the external environment. This could be likened to looking in the mirror while eating. Confluence is represented by an infinity sign over the self–environment boundary signifying a closed system which effectively destroys the function of the boundary. This can be likened to suckling at the breast or what some teenagers graphically refer to as 'sharing spit' (kissing).

Boundary Disturbances (or Interruptions) in Detail

Desensitisation (Minimising Sensation)

In 'desensitisation', the neurotic avoids experiencing himself or the environment. The concentrating self feels anaesthetised and deadened. This is where sensations and feelings of the self are diluted, disregarded or even neglected. The existence of pain or discomfort is kept from emerging as figure in varying degrees. A mild example is lying in the sun too long. A more extreme example is disregard of bodily needs – such as in the kind of people who take pride in how much they can drink, go without sleep and work under extreme stresses such as on the stock market – whilst taking no account of the toll this lifestyle is taking on their health and on their hearts.

Desensitisation may occur at any phase of the awareness cycle; for example a very thirsty person, whilst swallowing a much-needed drink, may in the final contact phase desensitise against the kinaesthetic relief because of watching the news on television. Desensitisation is discussed in this book as an interruption during the sensation phase of the cycle.

A certain level of desensitisation may be part of healthy living; for example, an athlete might ignore the irritation of a small blister in order to win a race, or someone may ignore the discomfort of a lumpy mattress to attain some sleep.

Deflection (Avoiding Sensation or Meaningful Impact)

'Deflection' means to turn aside from direct contact with another person. It is a way of reducing one's awareness of (the impact of) environmental contact, making it vague, generalised or bland. The subject-matter may be subtly changed, for example, the woman asks – 'Do you love me?' The man answers – 'What do you mean by love?' Instead of sharing direct feelings with their full emotional intensity the client chooses abstract language, watered-down descriptions or avoids eye contact. A person who habitually deflects does not use his or her energy in an effective way in order to get feedback from self, others or the environment. Perhaps no criticism can 'get through' but neither can appreciation or love.

> The deflecting person doesn't reap the harvest from his activity. Things just don't happen. The person may talk and yet feel untouched or misunderstood.

His interactions misfire, not accomplishing what he might reasonably expect. Even though an individual may communicate validly or accurately if he doesn't reach *into* the other person he won't be fully felt. (Polster and Polster, 1974: 90–91)

In deflection, the neurotic tries to avoid the impact of stimuli from himself or the environment. The concentrating self feels alienated and abandoned.

Deflection is usually harmful and metaphorically strips the flavour from rich and vivid contacts. However, there are times when deflection can be very useful as a survival manoeuvre in situations which are potentially dangerous. For example, the deflection of propaganda or misinformation in a totalitarian state can be most useful and result in better contact with the true situation in the long run. Deflection may interrupt any part of the cycle but especially distracts from a person's awareness.

Introjection (Being Ruled by Internalised 'Shoulds')

'Introjection' is the initial mechanism by which we take in food, ideas and rules from significant others in our environment. Until the baby cuts teeth (a most significant developmental milestone for Perls), it cannot easily eject in a discriminating way that which is bad (dysfunctional) for it other than by vomiting or spitting out. With the advent of dental aggression comes the potential to chew the information from our environment, to take in what is organismically important or nourishing and to differentially expel that which is not suitable. This capacity then applies to all sources of nourishment – food, relationships or information. 'In introjection, the neurotic justifies as normal what the concentrating self feels as an alien body it wants to disgorge' (Perls et al., 1951/1969: 463).

As children, people 'swallow' rules or borrow maxims such as 'you must always work hard', 'you must put other people's needs first', 'you must control your feelings at all times'. People may also swallow attributions whole – for example, 'you're the lazy one', 'you are more creative than your sister', 'all the men in our family end up as alcoholics'. People who habitually introject are nearly always 'cocking an ear' for or 'keeping an eye out' for what they *should* be doing. They lack an inner sense of self-directedness or self-regulation in terms of their own needs. Their introjects are alien to themselves, inflexible and totalitarian 'you should always . . .'. Cultural stereotypes, such as magazine portrayals of women as passive and willing objects for male consumption, are subtly introjected by vast numbers of people without them being aware that they are doing this.

Introjection which continues in adult life may occasionally be helpful in the initial phases of learning certain skills ranging from typing to modelling on one's own counsellor. In the ideal situation, later in the process, all the early rules will be re-examined to investigate their relevance and applicability for the person, the situation and the moment.

Introjection may interfere with any phase of the awareness cycle. For example, a woman may enjoy sex but not allow herself an orgasm (final contact phase) because of introjected messages like 'sex is only for men to get relief'. However, introjection often interferes profoundly with mobilisation, preventing the person from taking appropriate action to meet his or her needs.

Projection (Seeing in Others what I Don't Acknowledge in Myself)

A projection is a trait, attitude, feeling, or bit of behavior which actually belongs to your own personality but is not experienced as such; instead, it is attributed to objects or persons in the environment and then experienced as directed *toward* you by them instead of the other way around. The projector, unaware, for instance, that he is rejecting others, believes that they are rejecting him; or, unaware of his tendencies to approach others sexually, feels that they make sexual approaches to him. (Perls et al., 1951/1969: 211)

Projection can be used in healthy and constructive ways in planning or anticipating future situations. All kinds of creativity involve some projection of the self into the work of the imagination. Sometimes people see fine qualities such as honesty or intelligence in others without being able to acknowledge that they already possess these qualities too. Cases of projection may provide the basis for the folk wisdom – 'it takes one to know one'.

Prejudice is a particularly subversive and destructive kind of projection. Disowned aspects of the self are attributed to the despised race or class or sex, thereby relieving the onus on the projector to come to terms with his or her own shadow qualities. There is often a grain of truth in a projection but frequently such people are paying very selective attention to the environment or experiencing themselves as powerless to change the situation. Although projection may occur as an interruption of any part of the awareness cycle, it may often be seen as a disturbance to the action phase.

Retroflection (Doing to Myself Instead of to the Other)

'Retroflection' means 'to turn sharply back against'. There are two types of retroflection – the first is when the person does to herself what she wants to do to or with someone or something. This probably derives from what she originally did or tried to do to other persons or objects. The personality is split into the aspect who 'does' and the aspect that is 'done unto'. Instead of expressing the aggressive impulse towards the hurtful parent, such people turn the aggressive impulse in upon themselves and live a life of self-castigation with inwardly directed hostility, and may eventually commit suicide, which is the retroflective form of homicide. 'In retroflection, the neurotic is busily engaged where the concentrating self feels left out, excluded from the environment' (Perls et al., 1951/1969: 463).

People may learn to retroflect when their feelings and thoughts are not validated in their families of origin or when they are punished for the expression of their natural impulses. The impulse to hit out remains locked in the person's body, affecting muscular patterns, abdominal tension and chemical balances in the body. Energy is used to suppress the original held-back impulses, thereby also draining energy away from the person's capabilities of getting his or her needs met in the current environment.

Most of us are taught that aggression is bad, and the expression of our aggressive impulses may inevitably lead to destruction and damage. However, in Gestalt aggressiveness as defined in the original sense of 'reaching out' is indispensable to life, love and productive activity. A positive use of retroflection is restraining yourself from crying inappropriately in a committee meeting. It becomes negative when you *never* let yourself express your hurt or your rage.

Another kind of retroflection is when you do to yourself what you want or wanted to have done for you by others. A person may give to himself the attention, love and care which was not given by the original parents. For example, Barry often puts his hand inside his shirt to stroke his chest when he speaks about his loneliness. When he gives a voice to his hand, he hears himself consoling his 'inner child' in the way that he had wanted his cold and distant father to have done for him. When this does not interfere with getting their genuine interpersonal needs met in the present, this can be an important form of self-support. Retroflection *may* occur at any phase in the cycle, but may specifically interrupt the final contact phase.

Egotism (Blocking Spontaneity by Control)

'Egotism' in Gestalt is characterised by the individual stepping outside of himself and becoming a spectator or a commentator on himself and his relationship with the environment. This neurotic mechanism gets in the way of effective action to get one's needs met, and disturbs the good contact with the environment. An internal commentary about how much one is enjoying a walk in an autumn park can destroy the unself-conscious pleasure of being truly *in* the experience. 'In egotism, the neurotic is aware and has something to say about everything, but the concentrating self feels empty, without need or interest' (Perls et al., 1951/1969: 463).

Perls, Hefferline and Goodman describe 'the neurosis of the psychoanalysed' in their discussion of egotism (although of course it is not confined to any single approach), showing how this kind of self-conscious spectatoring can become a problem in itself. It occurs when the person adopts the system he has been exposed to and becomes its 'ideal product' – a well-adjusted 'genital character', 'self-actualising', etc. The insights have not been integrated or assimilated. They sit upon him like a new suit of unfamiliar shape and proportions. While he admires himself 'being himself' in the mirror, his life lacks true spontaneity, his appetites seem programmed and his work lacklustre.

Perls, Hefferline and Goodman, however, point out that normal egotism is an indispensable stage in any developmental process of elaborate complication and long maturation in order to avoid premature commitment and the need to discourage 'undoing' (Perls et al., 1951/1969: 456).

Egotism may occur at any phase in the cycle – for example, instead of mobilising on hearing her baby's crying a mother may spend time congratulating herself on her sharp hearing. Egotism often interrupts satisfaction as the person becomes more involved with herself in the process than fully experiencing her satisfaction. Egotism at the moment of contact with the environment prevents a person from truly giving or receiving. Thus it interferes with the feeling of being 'full' or truly satisfied. Chronic egotism may result in habitual personality patterns which are described as narcissistic personality disorders where a lack of empathy, a pervasive pattern of grandiosity and hypersensitivity to the evaluation of others becomes rigidified (Yontef, 1988).

Confluence (Dysfunctional Closeness)

'Confluence' is the condition where organism and environment are not differentiated from each other. The boundaries are blurred as between the foetus and the mother. Two individuals merge with one another's beliefs, attitudes or feelings without recognising the boundaries between them and the ways in which they are different. Between them they behave as if they are one person. Any emphasis on boundaries is experienced as threatening to the relationship if not to the survival of the person. Couples who have lived together for a long time may come to resemble each other, have similar tastes and 'think alike'. It is not infrequent that they speak in the royal 'we', as in 'We believe that state education is good enough for our children'. They have relinquished their basic desires for separateness and surrendered part of their personalities. The idea of conflict or any disagreement seems to them to threaten the very foundation of their relationship.

All boundary disturbances originally had a survival function. Equally confluence in the emotional and physiological field of the mother and the growing baby is a necessary and healthy part of the child's development. Some confluence in relationships can be beneficial – for example, empathic understanding of a partner's bereavement. Some confluence with the environment can be life-enriching and enhancing. For example, in a meditational peak experience, or in certain forms of expressive art such as painting, the loss of self boundaries can be crucial to the full richness of the experience. Then, in healthy contact, there is a letting go with confidence that such moments can recur.

As with all human solutions there needs to be an appropriate balance between confluence and boundary-keeping and boundary-making. Experiencing some confluence with our environment is occasionally necessary so that we can experience assaults on our planet as biologically significant to ourselves. But a permanent merging or enmeshment with 'the other', whether person or situation, leads to loss of self, to lack of satisfactory contact and ultimately to disintegration.

Confluence can also be seen as a defence against facing one's ultimate existential aloneness, the certainty of mortality and the fear of the void. Each person experiences this 'void' differently. 'For each patient the void has different meanings. For the compulsive it may be disorder, for some it is age and death, for the young woman it may be the loss of self in sexual climax, for the early schizophrenic it is the force destroying the ego' (Van Dusen, 1975b: 92).

In the person who seeks dysfunctional closeness or merging in relationships there is both the inability to tolerate difference in the other and
the unwillingness to discover the resources of the self. In a 'merged' partnership neither individual can develop fully. The caretaking person often
colludes with the apparent 'dependent' one to avoid dealing with his own
fears of dependency or abandonment. Confluence may also manifest as an
unhealthy mingling of self with the situation such as one's occupation.
Some counsellors over-identify with their work to the extent that the personal self and the professional role become indistinguishable. Not
surprisingly this can lead to burnout, disillusionment and despair.

> Confluence is a phantom pursued by people who want to reduce difference so
> as to moderate the upsetting experience of novelty and otherness. It is a pal-
> liative measure whereby one settles for surface agreement, a contract not to
> rock the boat. Good contact, on the other hand, even in the deepest of unions,
> retains the heightened and profound sense of the other with whom contact is
> being made. (Polster and Polster, 1974: 92)

Confluence may prevent the sensation function from emerging rhythmi-
cally and spontaneously in the cycle of experience. For example, as long as
mother remains in confluence with her newborn baby and attending to his
needs, the sharpness of her sensory discrimination about her own needs
will naturally be diminished. For a period this, of course, is necessary.
Prolongation of this confluence may contribute to depression or subsequent difficulties in resuming an active sex life with her husband.

Confluence may occur at any point in the awareness cycle, for example
at the sensation level, a pregnant wife may be having morning sickness and
her husband too feels ill. Confluence may be especially noticeable, as mentioned earlier in this chapter, as an interruption at the withdrawal stage of
the cycle. Chronic confluence is also a characteristic of people who are
sometimes described as chronic borderline personality disorders. Their
confluence may be erratic and unstable. Their intense and impulsive interpersonal relationships vary between confluence with an over-idealised
other and confluence with a devalued other. Their need to merge with
another person (all-nurturing alternating with all-rejection) needs careful
boundary-setting, an emphasis on responsibility and an integration of
apparent polarities (Yontef, 1988).

Some chronic interruptions to contact have been related to commonly
used diagnostic categories. There is no intent to suggest that real people

resemble their diagnostic descriptions. Examples have been provided more as a spur to discussion and dispute than as claims to veracity or accuracy. The counsellor using the Gestalt approach will be forever questioning the assumptions underlying the use of diagnostic categories. Equally, he or she will also regularly question the assumptions underlying the rejection of diagnostic categories. Gestalt-oriented counsellors develop their own understanding and practice from the creative tension between phenomenological description and clinical prediction. Neither of these types of Gestalten need be fickle or fixed.

Using the Interruptions in the Gestalt Counselling Process

Any of the interruptions can occur at any point in time on the experience cycle. So a counsellor must be prepared to work at all or any of the junctures. The beginning point of the counselling will be determined by where the client finds himself or herself at the start. It may be that the client has difficulty with mobilisation when there is a need to move toward a clear figure. This immobility then defines the starting point.

> Thus when a Gestalt therapist works with a client, he/she is indifferent both theoretically and practically as to where in the process the work is begun. The therapist is equally committed to work at all points in the cycle and, ultimately, to help the client experience with maximum fullness and clarity. (Melnick and Nevis, 1986: 45–6)

An understanding of the nature and sequence of the cycle of experience forms the basis in this book for considering how it can resemble the counselling process over time in some important dynamic ways. The function of boundary disturbances and their effects as impediments at different stages of this natural flow will be referred to throughout the discussion. Although the focus will be on the role of certain interruptions at certain phases, please bear in mind that these are for purposes of example and discussion, not definition or prescription. The next chapter will deal in some depth with the necessary preconditions for counselling, likening it to working at the sensation part of the experience cycle.

5

SENSATION AND THE
NECESSARY PRECONDITIONS
FOR COUNSELLING

> The story is told of a Zen monk who wept when he heard of the death of a close relative. When one of his fellows commented that it was unseemly for a monk to show such personal attachment, he replied: 'Don't be stupid! I'm weeping because I want to weep.'
>
> (Watts, 1962/1974: 155)

Chapter 4 contains a discussion of the stages of Gestalt formation and destruction and of boundary disturbances which may occur at any stage. As can be seen from Figure 4.1, for the purposes of this book a particular boundary disturbance is being discussed in conjunction with a particular phase in the cycle of Gestalt formation and destruction. It is, of course, understood that any of the boundary disturbances may occur at any other stage in the cycle of Gestalt formation and destruction. However, in this book this particular organisation will be used to represent static moments or punctuation marks of an ongoing process. This device can only poorly approximate the dynamic kaleidoscope of the Gestalt of the counselling process with its infinite variability.

The next six chapters of the book will be organised to correspond with the stages of the cycle as they can reflect the developmental phases of the counselling process. Each chapter will focus on another developmental phase in the sequence of the counselling process and link it to stage-posts on the Gestalt cycle and potentially corresponding disturbances. Each chapter will contain: firstly, a general discussion of each of the *stages* in the Gestalt cycle of experience related to the counselling process; followed by a discussion of typical *issues* which occur at these stages; and finally, a presentation of some *techniques* or experiments specifically related to the boundary disturbances which may often match the particular phase in the cycle. (These may also occur in a related form at other stages in the cycle.) These experiments or techniques are not meant to be used as techniques per se. Even where it may sound as if answers are being given or counsellor-responses being prescribed, the best kind of Gestalt is devoid of deliberated 'techniques'. The intent is that these examples of interventions be used questioningly and adapted for general application, particular stages in the counselling process or with the different types of personality (using the different boundary disturbances). The strategy to be used by the counsellor can never be prescribed in Gestalt. These so-called procedures or experiments are examples of spontaneous inventions of previous counselling/client dyads and are here intended as *provocations* to discovery, invention and creativity.

Establishing Sensation Function

There are certain preconditions which need to exist in order for the counselling relationship to be possible at all. Gestalt is largely a verbal approach to human distress, so a minimum ability to communicate by words is desirable. However, it is not always necessary. Some Gestaltists, for example, work with brain-damaged clients, facilitating their sensory perceptions and bodily experiences by using media such as rhythm and music. Indeed, it is important to remember that the very concept of self-actualisation was contributed by Goldstein (1939). He postulated this as the sovereign motive of the organism (person) and saw all other drives or needs (for example, erotic or aggressive needs) as derivatives thereof. Goldstein developed this idea in working with brain-injured soldiers. It remains a guiding vision in working with Gestalt, whatever the capacities of the client.

Gestaltists always pay attention to the body, and some may even have had training in therapeutic massage or body work. Gestalt practice is always fundamentally based in what the counsellor can see, hear, feel and smell about the client, rather than in what the counsellor thinks, interprets or understands about the client. The stress is on awareness. This emphasis on the primacy of the senses was Perls's reaction against the over-intellectualisation of the counselling process as can happen in more primarily cognitive or psychoanalytic approaches. It was never meant to exclude the thinking function of Gestalt practitioners. Perls wished to emphasise the enormous but neglected importance of such pre-judged, pre-interpreted, pre-classified sense data in developing a counselling relationship. This is the phenomenological core of Gestalt – a philosophical attitude of openness to experience which is reflected in the practice of putting the person's subjective experience first. Such a relationship of mutuality exists when client and counsellor are partners in the counselling process. Then they can work together, in contrast to situations where the expert 'understands' more about the client's psychology than the client himself. Gestalt fosters autonomy, with the use of support of course, but with eventual interdependence as a goal and as a present possibility.

In the Gestalt cycle of experience, the task is to enable the person to move from the completion of the withdrawal stage through the void of fore-contact to sensory responsiveness in a way which is most growthful for that person. An extremely damaged person who can no longer register pain, and bangs his head against a wall until it bleeds, has become desensitised to the pains and discomforts of ordinary human life to the extent where his survival is threatened. The very act of self-mutilation, whether it be self-inflicted cigarette burns, cut wrists or prolonged starvation, is often the person's desperate attempt to re-establish the organismic sensation function. States of hypnosis, hysterical conversions, trauma after-effects or sleep deprivation may temporarily mimic dis-association from sensation. Although counsellors are not generally expected to deal with catatonic schizophrenia or stuporous depressions it is important that counsellors be familiar enough with such syndromes so that they can be alert for early signs of them, and have the necessary access to psychiatric colleagues should containment, advice and/or medication become necessary. On a much smaller scale temporary states of withdrawal, with some loss of sensation function, may occur at times in an ordinary counselling session, particularly after a deeply emotional piece of work or a new insight.

There are other examples of people who have become alienated from their senses and where, no matter how luxurious and enticing the stimuli, they no longer respond with genuine discrimination or pleasure. This may be the bored, blasé, world-weary emptiness of the narcissistic personality who 'has seen and experienced it all'. It may also be the client who compulsively seeks out sexual thrill after sexual thrill, needing each one to be more bizarre and perverse than the preceding one.

Both client and counsellor need to become familiar with empty spaces in their life experience, learn to tolerate them and to transform them through exploration from 'futile voids' to 'fertile voids'. This requires a willingness to stay in a state of confusion and uncertainty, as well as the responsibility for 'moving on' when the time is ripe. Then sensation can be allowed to emerge as a figure from a ground which is at the same time both empty and chaotic with possibilities and potentials.

Counselling work at the sensation juncture of the awareness cycle is often slow and painstaking. The relationship has to be built with many small steps focusing on the minutiae of experience.

> The creative therapist must find a way to insert himself into that part of the person's experience which is still alive, still perking. From there he teaches the client, through directing his awareness, to anchor himself in the environment. This may include the person's awareness of his body, its weight on the chair, its position in space, its minute sounds and movements. (Zinker, 1978: 99–100)

Of course, an acute aliveness of sensation function in the counsellor is essential for useful assessment of a client and the ground from which experience can grow. Psychiatrists of Kraepelin's generation used to say that they could smell schizophrenia. It is important even for the beginning counsellor to learn to become acutely sensitive to clients who are potentially violent, suicidal or psychotic. The preliminary rough outlines of treatment are often presented in overture form at the very first contact and, as such, may influence the subsequent course of the counselling whether the counsellor is aware and intentional about such early sensory information or not. In an ultimate sense the counsellor's truest ally is his or her intuition. To the extent that this intuition is informed or educated it can become a reliable asset.

Diagnosis and Planned Treatment

Modern Gestaltists are reclaiming diagnostic acumen and usefulness, albeit within a phenomenological frame (Clarkson, 1988). However, the idea of planning and structure in Gestalt was already in the seminal techniques of Perls by the late 1940s. 'As soon as the structure of the neurosis is clear to the therapist, he should plan his course of action, but remain alert and elastic during the whole treatment' (Perls, 1979: 21). I believe this still applies. Of course, it involves knowing what the counsellor can and cannot work with and this, in turn, depends specifically on the counsellor's training, personality, experience, resources and ability to diagnose, estimate probabilities and assess clients and their situations accurately, yet sensitively and *existentially* from the very beginning.

Attitudes towards diagnostic work in Gestalt are as usual extremely varied, ranging from vehement refusals to take psychiatric terms seriously at all, to complex and highly developed systems linking DSM IV (*Diagnostic and Statistical Manual*) personality disorders, diagnoses with the cycle of awareness, contact functions, resistance mechanisms and support systems, as well as basic polarities and self-image (Delisle, 1988).

For the purposes of this introductory book I would rather encourage counsellors to develop their own approaches to integrating perception, recognition and prediction.

By combining initial impressions, subjective responses, and an openness to the existential encounter, counsellors can use the boundary disturbances and stages of the awareness cycle to develop and plan their counselling, as long as the paradox of diagnostic description and possibility of change can be held as alternating figure and ground for each other. Each person is unique. After all, counselling is an attempt to change diagnosis, whether it be a label of 'obsessive–compulsive' or a self-imposed limitation such as 'I am always anxious in new situations'.

For this book I suggest one map in which counselling sequences can over time be conceptualised alongside particular boundary disturbances. On the basis of the characteristic boundary disturbance occurring at the most frequently interrupted part of the cycle, dynamically alive descriptions become possible which draw on the unique constellations as they apply in every individual case. For example, a person who chronically projects suspicion, disapproval and malice may do so more acutely at the withdrawal phase of the contact cycle. Treatment planning will follow from such an approach in an organismically unfolding way.

Typical Issues of the Preliminary (Sensation) Phase

Setting the Stage

The counselling environment in Gestalt frequently reflects some of the values of the approach. There is usually comfortable furniture including cushions which can be used symbolically. Space in which the client can move, walk or dance is desirable, since full body expression does not accord well with a restricted environment. A sensorily rich and interesting milieu can be created by paintings, pot-pourri, lighting, etc. For clients who need to be enlivened in terms of their sensation function, such factors can be very important therapeutically. The provision of soft toys, clay, coloured pens and paper, or a sand tray with a variety of objects easily available, enhances possibilities for available symbolic enactment or fantasised resolutions.

Gestalt encourages free and full expression of emotions when this is organismically timely, safe and necessary for the person. Therefore the management of noise is a significant feature for a counsellor using the Gestalt approach. Clients need to be in a room or environment where they can weep or rage loudly without having to worry that the neighbours might call the police. Confidentiality and privacy are prerequisites for clients to begin to have good enough support for self-exploration.

The environment or consulting room is also important for the counsellor. To work alone in an empty office or house with potentially violent clients is both irresponsible and possibly counterproductive for the client. The proximity of colleagues, alarm systems and fire extinguishers may seem irrelevant to many beginning counsellors, until the occasion arises where pre-planning could have avoided catastrophe.

The Gestalt counsellor needs to be aware of making good and clear contact with a prospective client from the first telephone call or meeting. A counsellor who models behaviour at gross variance with her professed values will not be trusted. But Gestalt practitioners vary enormously in individual style. Intake procedures in the Gestalt approach can be as traditional as psychiatric mental status examination, or as unorthodox as full engagement in the re-enactment of a trauma at a first session. Assessment for suitability in working with a Gestalt approach is a delicate process thoroughly grounded in intuition. Gestaltists will early on establish whether a client would be willing to work with the self-responsibility model. This is perhaps the most important single criterion.

Another vital ingredient in setting the stage is the *person* of the counsellor, particularly his or her motivation for wanting to engage in the work of counselling. My first psychoanalyst used to say that there is only one kind of person attracted to this kind of work – people with emotional problems of their own. And then there are two kinds of people who stay in this kind of work – those who deal with their problems and those who don't!

This wry comment reflects an appreciation of the profound mixture of motivations that may influence people in choosing counselling as their occupation. The situation is no different in Gestalt. The safeguard for counsellor and client alike lies in the profound and expensive commitment to their personal growth, psychotherapy, training and supervision which should form part of the prerequisites for any counselling activity.

Severely Disturbed Clients

Although this book is not written for counsellors who are working primarily with severely disturbed clients, counsellors should know about profound forms of mental and emotional disturbance in order to recognise potential signs thereof at an intake interview. Counsellors should also be able to deal with such manifestations if and when they occur later in the counselling process, when the relationship is already well established. Such occurrences, where clients go into suicidal or psychotic episodes, are not at all impossible in any ordinary practice, no matter how carefully the selection procedure has been done. In fact, apparently well-functioning clients often need to plummet to the deepest layers of their despair or their 'madness' in order to emerge from their 'dark night of the soul.'

Gestalt, although most popularly associated with the growth processes or treatment of mental health professionals, has also been found to be useful as a conceptual framework and treatment methodology for people who have been labelled psychotic. Even though this may not be part of a counsellor's practice, studying the work of authors such as Stratford and Brallier, 1979; Gagnon, 1981; and Van Dusen, 1975a, will indubitably enrich a counsellor's understanding and appreciation of the value of Gestalt in dealing with severely disturbed individuals.

Somatic and Medical Problems

It is usually necessary to take into account people's dietary habits, their rest and sleep cycles and their current medication when assessing their suitability for counselling. For example, there is considerable research evidence which indicates that many clients are treated for symptoms of anxiety when, in fact, they are physiologically and psychologically reacting to the effects of caffeine in coffee (Lee et al., 1985). A cessation of coffee drinking can result in a dramatic amelioration of the anxiety symptoms. It is imperative to take a full and complete medical history to avoid the kind of situation (which actually happened) where a counsellor kept working on a client's 'angry headaches', neglecting to involve medical practitioners. The client eventually died of a brain tumour whilst still in the care of the counsellor concerned.

Third-party Contacts

A frequent problem for a new counsellor occurs when he or she is first approached by a friend or relative of a person whom that friend or relative thinks should be in counselling. From people's concern about their loved ones they may even go so far as to suggest that the counsellor 'come to dinner with us so that my husband can get to meet you and begin to trust you, and perhaps then he would be willing to go into counselling about his drinking problem'. Usually a counsellor with a Gestalt approach would not take up such an invitation, since Gestalt is both philosophically and therapeutically predicated on the understanding that people can be responsible for their own choices. To commence the counselling relationship in either a dishonest or misleading manner would be contrary to the very spirit of Gestalt. Some counsellors may use this as an opportunity to explain the nature of responsibility and the way in which they work, but insist that the person concerned contacts the counsellor directly. Another option (among many) is to suggest conjoint work, where both parties to the *system* can work together and discover how they mutually maintain the dysfunction. For example, there are many accounts in clinical lore of alcoholics whose wives leave them when the husbands stop drinking, thus suggesting that the husband's drinking also served a function for the wife. This is one illustration, among many, of the importance of taking into account the client's material or social systems as part of the field of endeavour.

Many counsellors do not take on clients who are drug-addicted or alcohol-addicted, unless the counsellors have special training or work in special units where they can use Gestalt effectively and successfully with such clients.

Cultural Factors

Cultural factors also need to be taken into consideration when taking on new clients. It is possible that, for example, an Asian client might prefer to be referred to an Asian counsellor, or a male homosexual might prefer a counsellor who is male and homosexual. It is not the intention of this book to treat this important matter in any depth. However, it is vital that all counsellors consider, and continue to reconsider, the influence of their values, their social class, their religious, political or sexual attitudes on their counselling practice.

Gestalt is a humanistic psychological approach which involves a conscious and intentional use of values in the counselling process. Gestalt practitioners, on the whole, do not profess neutrality towards client issues about which they have strong values. This will be different for different Gestaltists. A Gestalt practitioner I know has refused to take on a man who came wanting help with a weight problem while pursuing a spare-time practice of hounding and beating up Pakistani children on the estate where he lived. In another instance a man, complaining of severe depression while maintaining an incestuous relationship with his fourteen-year-old daughter, refused to see any link between these two aspects of his life, and adamantly maintained that it was not harming her and that he would not stop. The counsellor refused him treatment and reported him to social services.

Counsellors need to be in concordance with legal and ethical practice wherever they may work, or be aware of the consequences of alternative choices. Their own autonomous considerations may lead to occasions where counsellors make decisions according to the higher demands of their consciences. For example, counsellors who work in the army or in Roman Catholic settings may face conflicts of value. Hopefully, such problematic situations will also benefit from consultations with supervisors.

Specific Procedures

Desensitisation is a frequent boundary disturbance in the beginning phase of counselling (here corresponding to sensation). It is very likely to be operational in cases of severe dysfunction, deprivation or situations where other professionals may need to be involved. However, it is also relevant in all cases where people have become alienated from their sensations.

Knowledge of Emergency Procedures and First Aid

In serious and acute crises it is important that the counsellor know how to administer first aid and can rapidly contact the emergency services. In other situations the Gestalt practitioner may be part of an emergency or hospital team where all skills, experience and information come into play.

All counsellors should know and be proficient in basic first aid procedures such as mouth-to-mouth resuscitation, should learn the Heimlich manoeuvre (useful in cases of choking), the recovery position (useful in, for example, fainting, recovery from epileptic fit), etc. The counsellor may use such a skill perhaps only once in a professional lifetime. Having the skill then will make it worthwhile. It also maintains the counsellor's confidence and authority in day-to-day work.

Co-operation with Other Professionals

In considering any client for a longer-term counselling relationship the possible involvement of other professionals must be taken into account. Professional practice guidelines require that counsellors do not see clients who are in treatment with other counsellors/psychotherapists or psychiatrists without consulting colleagues. Co-operation with medical colleagues can provide appropriate psychiatric consultation and emergency back-up services such as medication, or help with admission to hospital. Developing relationships with other professionals who may be or become involved (be they social workers, marriage guidance counsellors or homeopaths) will usually reduce the chances of the client pitting one professional against another, make subsequent negotiations more fruitful and perhaps open up creative ways of collaboration which can be to the benefit of all concerned.

When Olive was first referred to me she was barely able to put one foot in front of another due to the severe motor retardation which accompanied her depression. Her speech was severely impaired and she was unable to follow any train of thought to its conclusion without drifting off into reverie. She was a middle-aged widow who lived alone for several years, ignored by her children and progressively deteriorating. Neighbours eventually called in her general practitioner; the doctor prescribed anti-depressant medication and suggested she consult a counsellor. Physiologically and psychologically she was too deprived to engage fully with me. Indeed I could not provide human touch of the quality and quantity which she had come to need within the counselling framework. I suggested to her that she get massaged two or three times a week by a qualified and ethical practitioner near her home, in addition to seeing me for regular appointments. Gradually her depression lifted. As her life force regained strength in her body under the healing ministrations of the masseuse, her ability and willingness to engage verbally with me on the journey of self-discovery developed.

Sensory Grounding

James was referred after having been physically attacked by an adolescent in the hostel where he worked. Prior to this assault he had built up a relationship of liking and trust with the young person, pleading for her with the head of the unit when her expulsion was being considered. Thus he was already in a state of shock on arriving at the counsellor's rooms and rapidly started to 'relive' the horrifying event in the way that post-traumatic clients such as rape and accident victims often do. Towards the end of the session, though, he appeared to have difficulty regaining his ordinary consciousness. Techniques, questions or physical involvement which help clients to 'ground' themselves in their senses, may often help to re-orientate people after severe shock. Using his name firmly and clearly, while touching him lightly on the shoulder established some vague recognition. Simple questions such as 'What is your name?'; 'What is the colour of my shirt?' and 'How many paintings can you see on the wall?' can be used. Later, simple instructions to attend to sensory input like: 'James, stand up'; 'Keep breathing' and 'Feel the skin on your right hand', may be helpful depending on the relationship, the context, the person and the counsellor's diagnostic acumen.

Using Creative Media

For people who are not very articulate, the use of creative media such as collage, finger painting, sand-tray work or puppetry can become a method of communicating, and can establish the beginnings of allowing the counsellor to become significant or impactful. It can also be the vehicle for a dialogue to develop in the relationship.

Davy was a thirty-year-old labourer who had difficulty ejaculating during intercourse with his wife. As a boy he had been humiliated and teased by schoolmates and teachers alike. Communication between counsellor and young man happened largely through his drawings on large sheets of paper, since he had but a limited vocabulary and little facility for talking about his feelings. On one particular occasion, for example, he drew a schoolyard scene and the counsellor asked whether she could join in using the space of the sheet which Davy had obviously left free. She drew angry, black clouds. He ended the session by symbolically setting fire (in bright orange and red colours) to the schoolyard and then tore the drawing into shreds. Delightedly he looked up. For the first time in his life he had asserted his aggression in his own defence – even if symbolically – and directed it against the humiliations of his past. This marked a turning point for Davy in his relationship with his wife, and a cessation of the problem. It is highly likely that there was more counselling work to be done. However, he had only asked for a six-session contract and had achieved the goal he came for.

The use of creative media is, of course, also potentially very liberating for people who are extremely articulate and who have become used to analysing their feelings away or desensitising their emotions through intellectualisation or compulsive verbal duelling. Dan, a professor of philosophy, was used to elegantly arguing his way around the complexities of the logical positivists while he had a growing sense of the meaninglessness of his own life. Sitting on the floor and using playdough to represent the void and emptiness inside him became his route to self-rediscovery.

Re-establishing the Pleasure Response

In situations such as dealing with people who are suffering severe clinical depression following months under torture or other cases of 'anhedonia' (lack of pleasure) the counsellor with a Gestalt approach needs to be creative and unafraid to experiment with the unusual. One Gestaltist I know takes such clients out into the garden and sets up opportunities to play with them games they loved in childhood. Alternatively she sometimes creates new and novel experiences by physically accompanying them to a funfair, circus or an especially wonderful delicatessen.

The Self of the Therapist as Instrument

In the moment before the first meeting with the client there are many questions for a counsellor with a Gestalt approach. Most importantly – where can I begin in contacting this person? How can I open myself to this new person as we begin our dialogical relationship? According to Hycner, this

> requires walking the 'narrow ridge' between responsibility *for* and responsibility *to*, other persons. It is quite likely that such a stance initially requires taking responsibility *for* the initiation of a genuine dialogical relationship, but that is done only to help establish (or re-establish) a genuine relatedness. Within that atmosphere, both client and therapist are better able to take full responsibility for themselves. (Hycner, 1985: 34)

Any existential therapy, such as Gestalt, emphasises the presence of the whole person of the therapist. 'This emphasis on the manifest presence of the therapist as a person in therapy is one of the most important differences between Gestalt therapy and psychoanalytic approaches with their analytic stance. The Gestalt therapist shares observations, affective responses, prior experience, creativity, intuition, etc.' (Yontef, 1988: 25). Yontef stresses, however, that all 'sharing' of personal experience by the therapist needs to be done within the most useful sequence of exploring the most central issues with good timing.

Authenticity does not mean belabouring clients with 'honesty' and 'self-disclosure' without regard for *their* needs, developmental levels, or personal readiness. A Gestaltist is spontaneously and authentically different with different clients and at different stages of the counselling process.

This obviously requires that the personhood of the helper be nourishing rather than toxic, as free as possible from projecting her own past unfinished business at the client, and be at the same time self-supporting as well as open to challenge, exploration and support from others. Gestalt-oriented counselling develops within a relationship as a whole which includes many isolated here-and-now moments as well as an indivisible continuity over time (Yontef, 1987).

One of the aims of this book is to illustrate how the overall counselling process can be a reflection of the Gestalt awareness cycle. In service of this goal certain of these issues or problems which may occur at certain phases of the counselling process will be briefly discussed. Of course the highlighted issues or problems may also occur or recur at any of the other phases. Equally other problems or issues may be foreground for a particular client/counsellor partnership, since there is no way of expecting human beings, much less the counselling relationship, to follow clockwork sequences. In each section this is followed by a discussion or description of experiments or techniques which may be particularly useful then, or at other times in the counselling relationship.

In the next chapter the beginnings of the counselling relationship and the function of awareness will come under the spotlight.

6

AWARENESS AND THE INITIAL PHASES OF THE COUNSELLING PROCESS

Tenno, having passed his apprenticeship, had become a teacher. One rainy day wearing wooden clogs and carrying an umbrella he went to visit Nan-in. On greeting him, Nan-in said: 'I suppose you left your wooden clogs in the vestibule. I want to know if your umbrella is on the left or the right side of the clogs.'

Tenno was confused and could give no instant answer. He realised that he was not yet able to carry his Zen (awareness) every minute of the day. He subsequently became Nan-in's pupil and studied a further six years towards enlightenment.

(Reps, 1971: 43)

Awareness of Discomfort – Dealing with the Presenting Problems

It is almost always difficult to isolate beginnings in human processes. Most events seem to be linked with events that went before which appear to be connected with the events that preceded those. Gestalt is particularly sensitive to this systemic interrelatedness as a result of the influence of the field theory of Kurt Lewin (1952). To ask clients to begin at the beginning may be an impossible task. Whenever they (or we as counsellors) choose to begin is a beginning itself – even when an up-to-the-minute account on the current state of the marital relationship is the initial exchange. However we punctuate the temporal complexity of human lives, beginnings are often where awareness is freshest, most poignant and unprejudiced. It's the first impression of warmth in the eyes as the person walks in that can form the basis of trust in the relationship. It is the defensive holding pattern in the chest that comes to awareness most sharply, often before it has been analysed, understood or interpreted. Certainly we can acknowledge that the decisions which lead to a person becoming aware that he or she wants to seek counselling are very complex, and have probably been made and remade many times.

In our culture it is an accepted part of education that children be taught how to brush their teeth, keep their bodies clean and many get detailed instruction in the area of sexual relationships. What the school curriculum frequently neglects is issues of emotional education such as how to cope with failure or how to deal with feelings of anger, fear and sadness. It is not culturally expected that children should 'naturally' know how to prevent tooth decay. It *is* expected that they should 'naturally' know how to prevent the decay of their curiosity, spontaneity and spirit. People who see the dentist regularly are held up as examples. People who 'break down and cry' are looked upon as 'sissies' or weaklings. There is still a social stigma attached to taking emotional care of yourself or to seeking information about how people function as emotional beings. So a certain amount of deflection (particularly awareness of sexual and emotional sensations) is culturally conditioned and even rewarded, whereas awareness (of pain, of fear) can be seen as weakness.

Wendy had a basic feeling of inadequacy and personal unacceptability ever since she was born to a teenage mother whose social standing and career potentials were destroyed as a result of her pregnancy. Wendy was used to being told that she was unwanted, 'nearly ruined her mother's womb' and generally had to feel grateful for not being aborted. Mother dealt with her ambivalent feelings towards Wendy with resentment, escalating demands and incessant fault-finding.

Wendy sought counselling only after many attempts at 'self-help' had failed. A kindly teacher, women's magazines, and desperate attempts at 'self-improvement' had already failed many times. Hers was a problem of long-standing and chronic low self-esteem, depriving her life of light and joy and the spontaneity which could have been hers. Up to that point she had seen need for help as a further sign of her weakness and inadequacy. When Wendy actually asked for counselling it represented not an act of hope for her, but an act of despair – giving up on herself.

Richard, a forty-year-old accountant, sought counselling when his marriage of ten years broke up and he went into a severe depression which was accompanied by recurrent migraines. His wife was not clear why she finally found their marriage intolerable, but he was devastated by her accusations of his emotional absence and lack of intimacy. He even had some difficulty understanding what she meant. He had not been unhappy with the marriage, believed they had a good relationship and was not aware of any ongoing or incipient problem. As a very young boy he had been sent to boarding school, encouraged to 'behave like a man' and developed an appropriate social persona while his 'inner child' got lost. The awareness of discomfort for him came to his attention following the marital crisis, whereas for Wendy it always appeared to be part of her foreground.

Frederika's decision to come into counselling was not prompted by a long-standing dissatisfaction or a particular crisis, but by a growing awareness of a hunger to explore herself more fully and to develop her creativity and potential in ways which she had not so far done. She was attracted to Gestalt as a method because of its emphasis on creativity and spontaneity, its compatibility with her basically humanistic philosophy and also because it appeared to be fun and exciting. Several friends of hers appeared to have been 'freed' from many restrictions and inhibitions through counselling. In particular a friend who was a painter developed a new more vibrant style of painting, as well as increased enjoyment of the creative process in herself. In Frederika's case she is entering counselling as a kind of 'gratuitous creative act', creating a new situation for herself in order to encourage and facilitate her own growth. Gestalt is not only about problems or dysfunctions, it is also about a celebration of life.

Beginnings – Forming the Counselling Relationship

Each Gestaltist, as well as each client, will have particular preferences for beginning counselling. Some people rush into the relationship assuming intimacy and connectedness long before it has been established in a mutual way. Before true contact (which is not based on wholesale projection of past relationships or fantasised relationships) between two separate individuals can occur, some dialogue and some testing may be realistically necessary. It may be unwise or dangerous to 'trust' a counsellor (or anyone else such as a gynaecologist or lawyer) without first establishing their qualifications and professional standing.

For some people it has become a chronic and predictable pattern that they withhold themselves in the early stages of a relationship. For them the beginnings of the counselling relationship may be inordinately protracted.

Other clients rush into counselling in the same impulsive way they rush into relationships – without due care or protection for themselves. As a counsellor, the Gestaltist who habitually rushes in or habitually holds back is also operating from conditioned patterns and previous experiences, not allowing himself or herself to be open to the vivid newness of this encounter with this person.

Each Gestaltist will begin the counselling process uniquely anew with each client. What is useful and reassuring for one client (e.g. history-taking) can be unresponsive and destructive to another (e.g. one who needs/wants to unburden himself of a painful confession of having abused his daughter many years ago).

Here follows an example of how Jim Simkin (a celebrated Gestaltist) begins a therapeutic relationship with an inexperienced client:

> Good evening. I'd like to start with a few sentences about contract and then suggest an exercise. I believe that there are no 'shoulds' in Gestalt therapy. What you do is what you do. What I do is what I do. I do have a preference. I prefer that you be straight with me. *Please* remember, this is a preference, not a should. If you feel that you *should* honour my preference then that's *your* should! When I ask you, 'Where are you?' my preference is that you tell me – or tell me that you're not willing to tell me. Then our transaction is straight. Any time that you want to know where I am, please ask me. I will either tell you, or tell you that I am unwilling to tell you – so that our transaction will be straight. (Simkin, 1976: 18–19)

It is impossible to describe typical ways in which a Gestaltist would initiate the counselling relationship since there can be no prescription for existential meeting. Perhaps it is most important to start where the client is, to accept, value and respect the client's phenomenological truth. This means that his description or his assessment of his situation is taken for real, and the counsellor does not assume that there is another deeper truth or that the presenting problem covers the 'genuine problem'. This requires considerable discipline in the phenomenological attitude, particularly if the counsellor has had training which encouraged the model of an expert interpreter who understood more about the client's psyche than the client ever could.

The counsellor is more likely to model through his or her own behaviour a willingness, interest and serious commitment to engaging with the client as a collaborator in a mutual partnership of adventure. Even in the initial interview there is bound to be some combination of intervention or presence which combines that which is discomfortingly novel with what is reassuringly familiar. In this way the client can experience from the very beginning the stylistic range of the subsequent work and should have enough information by the end of the initial session to make a clear decision about the likely nature of the relationship with that particular counsellor. Client and counsellor will have a sense of whether their senses of humour match or collide, whether there is enough potential for trust and whether there is enough scope for surprise.

People tend to re-create their primary relational patterns with significant others, particularly counsellors, and the initiation of these can take a wide variety of forms. For example, there is often an expectation on the counsellor to somehow collude with or support a self-representation of powerlessness. This reflects the early impotence many people experienced as infants. It is crucial to Gestalt that clients understand even from the very beginning that they are now, as adults, responsible for the outcome of their work in counselling and ultimately that they are responsible for the quality of their lives. The artistry of the counsellor lies in finding the balance in every fresh moment between accepting the client's self-definition and presenting him with stimulation to an ever-widening range of choices. Indeed if the self is conceptualised as an ever re-creating here-and-now system of boundary contacts, personality can be said to be a description of one's current limitations and 'cure' the liberation of all potentials. Of course, beginnings are never over. After every session, or after every piece of work, there will be new beginnings, perhaps even new kinds of relationship with the counsellor.

Typical Issues of the Initial (Awareness) Phase

Trust/Distrust

The very idea that predictable issues may arise in some kind of sequence in the counselling process is in some way antithetical to the Gestalt approach. Such a structure may be experienced as an imposition and impediment to the spontaneous and (probably) atypical unfolding of each new healing partnership between counsellor and client. Keeping this danger in mind, however, can allow the confident Gestaltist to pay attention to the shifting figure/ground of idiosyncrasy and generality, of total uniqueness and commonly found human patterns.

Trust is that state of being during which people believe that their needs can be met without injury by others or their environment. Distrust is the conviction that the environment will be neither nourishing nor benign. This polarity is probably the most crucial in initiating and establishing a helping relationship. For clients who were abused and neglected in infancy or childhood the gift of trust can in itself already be a sign of lasting change to this damage. This is a biological necessity in terms of establishing firm support for the exploration which must apply to most people. So the beginning phases of counselling can be enormously helpful in establishing the trust which was absent during early development.

Helping and Being Helped

Another polarity which is highlighted in the counselling engagement is that of helping and being helped. On the one hand the Gestaltist encourages his clients to take full responsibility for their own feelings, life choices and behaviours. On the other hand it is necessary for clients to 'let the helper in' – to allow the counsellor to be helpful. For many people at this stage a focus seems to be the task of finding a balance between accepting help without collapsing and maintaining their autonomy in an interdependent relationship.

The spectrum of practice amongst Gestalt practitioners is exceptionally wide. In keeping with our orientation, based on creativity as fulcrum, the practice of any one Gestaltist may vary enormously from one situation to the next. There are limitations to static representation of such richness and diversity. It is true that most Gestaltists would make some form of contract with the client. There also seems to be a phase of learning how to be a client as much as learning how to get the best out of the counsellor. For the counsellor too these issues are alive in the current experience – 'can I allow this person to touch me?', 'will my engagement with this person change me?', 'what do I risk in forming this relationship with a client?' The fear of dependency and the wish for dependency are also very much a part of this initial phase. Of course this may recur, particularly at times when there is a deepening of the client's exploration or greater risks are being attempted at any other stage.

Another frequent polarity of motivation lies between the client's fear of being taken over by the beliefs and values of the counsellor on the one hand, and their wish for 'a system of beliefs' (whether psychoanalytic or Gestalt) which will provide them with security and certainty against the vicissitudes of life. People may fear losing their identity by joining an exclusive 'Gestalt club'. On the other hand they may long for a certain and reliable system of living that would be useful for all situations and also across all times. Such contrasting motivations emerge in all systems of counselling. Of course, ultimately the task is to find the true self which can both join and be independent, belong and separate, criticise and value. This necessitates the clarification of boundaries.

Boundaries and Identity

For people at the beginning of the kind of growth process that counselling can be, there is often confusion about boundaries between themselves and other people, themselves and their environment and within their bodies. A common example is Debbie, who doesn't know where in her body she actually experiences hunger. She eats when the clock says it's time, and when she is angry or tired or lonely. She complains that she has not experienced genuine hunger sensations for many years. To the extent that people are alienated from their physical selves they will interpret sensations falsely. This leads, as in Debbie's case, to anxiety being mislabelled as hunger. Clients then eat to still a displaced 'hunger' instead of attending to their anxiety but, as they do this, they become more alienated from their natural hunger and satiation cycles. Discovering where in her body she senses and experiences hunger pangs will make it more likely that Debbie will be able to experience her basic psychological and physiological needs and follow each one through the experience cycle to satisfaction and completion. One woman felt her 'stomach being very low down in her abdominal cavity'. Anatomically she was pointing to her lower intestines. She had believed this to be biologically accurate in an experiential way even though she had done biology at school and intellectually knew other facts to the contrary. This anatomical confusion reflected her confused awareness of her internal organs and hunger-satiation cycles.

Other boundaries that come into play are those of confidentiality and relationships with people in other social systems of the client such as their spouses, families and employers. All these people in the social system may in varying ways be simultaneously or alternately supporting the initiation of this special journey and (at least at some level) wishing to sabotage it. Perhaps they may feel threatened at their loved one's attempts at self-support and independence. For example, a mother rings the counselling centre in great distress about her twenty-four-year-old daughter who appears to have lost motivation for work or study, mopes around the house and suffers from anxiety, loneliness and despair. The daughter had had a relationship, had become pregnant, on mother's advice had an abortion and ended her relationship with her boyfriend. Mother complains that the daughter also believes that people talk about her behind her back.

The counsellor pointed out that by mother trying to make the appointment and establish a counselling relationship without the daughter's consent or participation, this is in fact true. The daughter's suspicions are indeed based on facts – but mother does not acknowledge this. Mother is used as the girl's confidante but she is also the person whom the daughter most profoundly resents and blames for the difficulty of her own life. Spouses are also well known for being in this ambivalent relationship at the start of counselling. They may be very supportive and want the person to engage in a change process, but as one of them said 'as long as she doesn't change in ways that I don't like.'

Since the Gestalt approach places such high values on one's responsibility for oneself, counsellors will only under exceptional circumstances deal with other members of the family, unless specifically requested to do so, for example in family therapy. Perls (1969b) shows the process of maturation as moving away from environmental support towards self-support. The person leaves and discovers first-hand for himself, instead of accepting the authority of others, and no longer depends on the praise or approval of others for his self-esteem.

Expectations and Fears

Much of the initial phases of the counselling process can be seen as a working-through of the client's expectation and fears. The polarity which can be most useful in conceptualising these parameters is that of abandonment or engulfment. For most people the earliest relationship with their primary caretaker (self/other boundary dynamic) can be characterised more by the one than by the other. In other words, baby and mother dyads can be described as having either boundaries which are too impermeable or boundaries which are too permeable. In the healthy mother/infant relationship there will be a rhythmic fluctuation depending on the infant's most urgent need at the time following the Gestalt cycle phases which we have already discussed. Unfortunately, because most caretakers have experienced some distortion of this healthy process in their own early experiences, they may pass on the early distortions or vigorously implement the opposite of what they received. For example, as a baby, Layla experienced her mother as engulfing her. Mother allowed her own needs to disappear while servicing Layla's every whim. Mother had no separate identity and lived through Layla's achievements, Layla's moods and her personality. Any independent activity on Layla's part, such as going to nursery school, mother experienced as a sad separation which confronted her over and over again with the emptiness of her own life. As a grown-up person, Layla developed all the features and problems of what has been described (Masterson, 1976) as borderline personality. When Layla in turn had a child she felt the enormous compulsion to repeat her mother's pattern with the baby by making the baby the centre of her universe. Through counselling Layla had achieved enough insight and understanding about how her mother's confluence had damaged her. So she took an opposite position with her baby daughter, avoiding holding her, creating long separations and generally guarding against the enmeshment in such an extreme form that the baby experienced emotional abandonment.

These opposite states of engulfment on the one hand and abandonment on the other have been described by Resnick (1987) in terms of confluence and isolation.

The earliest fears and expectations in the counselling relationship are likely to mirror the earliest fears and expectations of a person's life. The person whose early primary mode was confluence may tend to fear abandonment, for example that the counsellor may move to another city before completing the work. The person whose earliest primary mode was isolation, may tend to fear engulfment, for example that he or she may not be allowed to disagree or develop independently of the counsellor. Sometimes people may appear to be warding off engulfment as a means of avoiding experiencing the pain of their earliest abandonment. Sometimes people may appear to be warding off abandonment as a means of avoiding experiencing the violation of their earliest engulfment. The sensitive counsellor will be very alert to these characteristic relational modes and change his or her ways of working with a client, depending on how these polarities of abandonment or engulfment manifest in the counselling process.

Examples of Experiments

The techniques which follow can be viewed as also referring to ways and means of dealing with deflection – the boundary disturbance which is being used in this book to highlight the awareness phase of the Gestalt cycle as it may manifest itself in the counselling process.

Learning and Practising the Awareness Continuum

One of the most important skills that a Gestalt client can acquire is to follow his or her own 'awareness continuum'. It may appear a very simple process, yet in many ways it may take a lifetime to learn. Awareness has been defined and described earlier, in Chapter 3. The awareness continuum in this context is meant to refer to the ever-changing consciousness of moment-by-moment changes within oneself and in the environment. The Zen story at the beginning of this chapter illustrates the kind of failure of awareness which impedes full and effective functioning. Practice of the awareness continuum is a kind of training in applied phenomenology; an attempt to concentrate without judgement or labelling on every new figure which becomes of interest without preconception or expectation. Frequently human beings engage habitually in behaviours, attitudes and feelings stripped of conscious awareness. People eat, make love, go to work, etc. However, in all important ways they are unconscious or unaware of their here-and-now experiences, their recall is barren and their attention everywhere else but on the vividness of their life's every passing moment. The awareness continuum is particularly designed to heal this lack of 'mindfulness' and to restore richness and vitality to living.

It is emphatically not the same as introspection, because introspection splits the person into observer and observed. The technique of awareness means to maintain the sense of your actual existence from moment to moment. Practising the awareness cycle means excluding nothing – wishes, thoughts, bodily feelings, sensations from the environment, temperature changes, voluntary and involuntary actions and all these before judging or labelling or categorising. It is very similar to the Zen practice of 'mindfulness' and the way to get into this technique is to start verbalising without exception to every experience 'now I am aware . . .'

It is considered to be different from psychoanalytic free association in that it specifically includes all physical, mental, sensory, emotional or verbal experiences which form part of the unitary flow of experience. The Gestalt goal is to extend and increase integrated functioning of the body/mind self and to do it in awareness in the present. This includes bringing into conscious awareness what may otherwise remain un-conscious or out of awareness.

Using the Language of Responsibility

Gestalt is based on a fundamental assumption that people are responsible for their own feelings and behaviour as well as a philosophical commitment to the existential position which stresses the person's inalienable self-direction. This emphasis is carried through in the apparently small details of people's use of language. Perls, like Goldstein, emphasised that carelessness in speaking results in limitations of orientation and of action, and encouraged appreciation for the power of the word. Our choice of words and sentence construction is reporting and representing our inner world. In addition, from a systemic point of view it is also forming and influencing our current experiences and future attitudes. The way we speak is very often a highly accurate reflection of our inner processes and only rarely if ever coincidental. Our verbalisations mirror ourselves. Even apparent mistakes, as Freud pointed out, often bring to consciousness aspects to which we may otherwise not have paid attention.

The word 'personality' is derived from a root 'sonar' which means sound. So people who use the Gestalt approach to counselling also pay finely tuned attention to the quality and expressiveness or inhibition of people's natural sounds. In our use of language we can deny or assume responsibility and reinforce a position of powerlessness or self-direction from moment to moment. There is a world of difference between the subjective experience of the man who says: 'She made me so angry that I just had to hit her', and the man who says: 'I allowed her provocation to really get through to me'; the person who says: 'I suffer from indigestion' as opposed to 'I am giving myself a backache by tensing my neck muscles'. The phenomenological representation in language can thus reflect learned helplessness or intentionality. This assumption of responsibility, as mentioned earlier, is not to be confused with blaming, but is meant to emphasise personal agency and authorship for one's own life and experience.

In all cases what might seem a semantic difference is a very crucial stepping-stone in the counselling process. If it is you yourself tensing your muscles and creating a headache, then it is possible for you to become aware of how you are doing this. As you concentrate and attend to this process, the potential solution becomes available in the counselling consulting room between the counsellor and the client. If it is some mysterious germ that 'attacks you' or invades you against your will, and over which you have no influence at all, this creates an existential powerlessness which may be an equally viable philosophical assumption but is fundamentally de-powering and strips people of potential for changing their own reactions to situations.

Viktor Frankl (1964/1969) in his work *Man's Search for Meaning*, which Perls recognised as another form of *existential psychotherapy*, also stressed people's ability to choose their reactions in any given situation, even in situations which they have not chosen or engineered. What we may not have choice over is the situation, but we can choose how we want to respond to it. Frankl uses many examples of people in concentration camps, some of whom chose to become demoralised, betrayed their friends and the best part of themselves. Other people chose to react to these deplorable circumstances with self-respect, if not hope, and with a commitment to finding some meaning which would transform the squalor and misery of their everyday existence into something transcendent.

In Gestalt, therefore, clients are encouraged to experiment with construing their experience verbally in ways that demonstrate that they are taking responsibility for it. In some variants of Gestalt this has become another set of rote rules, for example, don't say 'It hurts', say 'I hurt'. Don't say 'You are hurting me', say 'I am hurting myself with your behaviour'. With such rote interventions the original intention has been lost, because then people may learn to say the right words but their experience is still that of an object upon whom life and other people act. To invite clients to change their language is to invite them into taking responsibility for themselves, not into following another set of instructions which are prescribed from the outside.

Exploring Non-verbal Behaviour

Gestaltists are usually vividly attentive to their own non-verbal behaviour and that of their clients. Crossed ankles, coughing, one shoulder being higher than another, are all important parts of the counselling process, especially as Gestalt attempts to encompass the whole person and seeks to integrate as many diverse aspects of that person as possible. Non-verbal behaviour can be explored by drawing it to the attention of the person, such as 'Are you aware that you blink your eyes much faster whenever you speak about your mother?'. Another way would be to ask people to exaggerate a particular movement, for example a gently kicking foot in the direction of the counsellor may, with such an invitation, bring to the awareness of the client his unexpressed anger at the counsellor. Seeing a video of themselves with the soundtrack deleted can be a fruitful experiential exercise for people to explore their own physical postures, non-verbal behaviour and attitudinal position in the world.

Redirecting Deflected Energy

Awareness is most profoundly disturbed by deflection – ways in which we reduce the impact of the environment on ourselves. Individuals may need to learn to re-direct their deflected energy by superficially simple manoeuvres such as making eye contact while talking about themselves. Some clients need to allow themselves to really make an impact on other people. One client said that she felt she had achieved this when she could reliably get service from a bartender in her due turn. In her past she usually was ignored while other people pushed in and got served before her. Clients may need to be encouraged to allow other people's communication and feedback, including their lovingness or appreciation, to really get through to them. Clara habitually complained that nobody appreciated her, yet when complimented she would regularly minimise thus: 'Oh it was nothing really.' As a child she was regularly ignored or blamed, so she never learnt to tolerate positive attention. By continuing to deflect such positive attention in her current life she of course perpetuates the fixed Gestalt of her past in her present relationships. Undoing deflection may require that clients relinquish deflecting mannerisms such as chewing gum, self-distracting body movements (twitching, finger rolling) or habitual facial expressions (frowning, blinking) which serve to reduce the quality of their awareness. When they become intensely aware of *how* they are creating the mannerisms, often the organismic need emerges. 'I roll my fingers in order to reassure myself that I am real'.

Many people do differential deflecting. They may accept all the positive things that people say about them but deflect any negative feedback. Other people only pay attention to negative feedback when it originates from envious or hostile sources, while deflecting appreciative recognition from reliable and trustworthy sources. Simple but important methods may include paying equal attention to positives, writing them down, repeating them to oneself. Deflection takes energy away from helping the person to get what he or she wants from life. Direct contact, whether with love or anger, food or physical exercise, enhances the quality of life and ensures that there are commensurate returns on the investment of time and energy. The deflected energy needs to be brought back on target and the person encouraged to get into direct contact with themselves, others and the environment. Circumlocution, abstract language or habitual self-denigration must usually stop in order for the person to feel that she is getting what she wants from life and that her rewards are commensurate with her investment of attention and energy.

Developing Sensory Awareness

For Perls it was important to differentiate between body, emotions and thinking. Most of us have lost large areas of sensory awareness and proprioceptive sensitivity in our bodies. These losses to our awareness often represent solutions to what at the time of suppression was an intolerable conflict, painful trauma or enduring deprivation. In counselling some of these archaic difficulties can be brought into awareness in a context of healing and authentic relationship. In this way the missing parts of the person as a body–mind whole can begin to be reclaimed.

> Concentrate on your 'body' sensation as a whole. Let your attention wander through every part of your body. How much of yourself can you feel? To what degree and with what accuracy and clarity does your body – and thus you – exist? Notice pains, aches and twinges ordinarily ignored. What muscular tensions can you feel? Attending to them, permit them to continue and do not attempt prematurely to relax them. Try to shape their precise limits. Notice your skin sensations. Can you feel your body as a whole? Can you feel where your head is in relation to your torso? Where are your genitals? Where is your chest? Your limbs? (Perls et al., 1951/1969: 86)

Perls defines neurosis as the extent to which there is a discrepancy between the verbal concept of the self and the felt awareness of the self. The best attitude for exploring this in yourself and in your clients is non-judgemental and curious experimentation. The development of sensory awareness in terms of smelling, tasting, listening, truly seeing and touching is not only therapeutic in the Gestalt approach but also essentially celebratory. Many people have been trained out of experiencing their natural taste or smell preferences in awareness, thereby depriving their experience of meaning, intensity and variety.

A very common outcome of the successful re-establishment of sensory and proprioceptive sensitivity is that people report awareness of pain whereas previously similar stimuli would leave them unaffected. Typically, a client reports 'I used to have a dentist drill my teeth without anaesthetic, but now it hurts too much'. The same applies to emotional sensitivity, particularly for people who learned to deny themselves a full range of emotional expressiveness as children, for example, under threat of bodily harm from abusing parents. They may become more sensitised to when people become insulting or injurious to them, whereas before counselling they might have let all such occasions pass. People may also become more attuned to the subtle manifestations of kindness, care and consideration which they receive from people in their environment: 'I never realised how friendly most people are when asked for help.'

Facilitating Transition

The first phase of counselling can be very satisfying for the client and counsellor alike, because of the focus on building or creating a relationship. Often this relationship, based as it is on respect for the person's basic health and organismic integrity, is the first in which the client feels truly validated as a person. For the counsellor too, this phase is gratifying. Most counsellors know how to establish relationships, and it is often their facility with this that attracts them to the profession. However, transition to another more demanding period may feel as though 'the honeymoon' is over. Many counsellors need training and supervision in helping them to make this transition to deeper and more difficult waters.

The Start of Gary's Journey

Gary had been living with Jessica for the past six years and he had found it very unsatisfactory for the last two of those years. Despite his growing discontent and frequent fantasising about how he could establish something better with someone different, he continued to stay with Jessica through fear of being alone, and guilt about hurting her. One afternoon on the university campus where he was a lecturer, he noticed an announcement about a forthcoming course of evening lectures on 'psychology for the lay person'. Psychology had been a field which he had until then regarded with suspicion, if not dislike. One of the lecturers mentioned on the poster was, however, someone he had previously heard speak on fields nearer his own, and he had found her highly lucid and interesting. Gary decided to attend these lectures. In the course of one of the evenings he learnt about third-force psychology and was fascinated by many of the ideas discussed, but in particular the idea of focusing on 'here-and-now-change'. His previous understanding of psychotherapy and counselling was largely based on media caricatures of a couch-bound patient endlessly ruminating about his past.

At the penultimate lecture he approached one of the lecturers (myself) and asked for a single counselling session – 'Just to look at whether or not I should leave my girlfriend . . . it won't take long.'

I made it clear to Gary that I would prefer not to see him for only a single session on such an important issue. We then agreed to spend a session exploring whether or not he in fact wanted to open a counselling relationship at that stage of his life.

At our initial session together, Gary arrived fifteen minutes early and when asked to wait he strode up and down the passage and looked relieved yet embarrassed when called into my consulting room. He sat in his chair with the lower part of his body sprawled and seemingly relaxed, yet his arms were fairly tightly folded across his chest and his right-hand fingers tapped a subtle tattoo on his left upper arm.

The vividness of these first impressions is characteristic of the naturally heightened awareness which attends beginnings. Many people can recall with exquisite detail beginnings they have experienced, and children are often fascinated by how their parents first met. In the same way the beginning of the counselling relationship is marked by a sensitisation of the counsellor and client to each other on a great many levels. With Gary I was aware of the colours, the quality and the texture of his clothes, including a pair of rather dirty trainers. I could smell that he was a smoker and that he used aftershave. He appeared to be 'weighing me up' in a similar way. My awareness of myself included experiencing a curious attention, a slightly increased heart-beat, and I was peripherally aware of the sound of April rain falling on the roof.

I verbalised some of my awareness of him, myself and our environment as a means of demonstrating the awareness continuum. I invited him to verbalise his awarenesses, whether they were intellectual, fantasy, visual, auditory, olfactory or whatever else. As he was doing this he became aware of wanting to force or seduce me into giving him 'an answer' to his current problem, but at the same time not wanting to trust or believe that anything that I had to say could really be of help to him.

Near the end of that first session Gary became aware of the sense of relief that accompanied his sharing with 'someone who needs no reciprocal care-taking' and he contracted to continue counselling on a weekly basis. During many of those initial sessions Gary would want to spend considerable time relating his past experiences to me. Sometimes my listening to him seemed appropriate and I learnt, for example, that another reason Gary feared separation from Jessica was because she would comfort him after his fairly regular nightmares. At other times I would interrupt his talking, especially if I became aware of some other process pressing for attention. An example of this happened one afternoon. The tone of Gary's voice became more and more 'droning' as he described a sticky period of his adolescent school life. I listened for a short while and then interrupted:

'Gary, stop for a while. I am experiencing your voice as sounding more and more boring and bored and wonder what's going on for you right now as you recount this part of your life story?'
'I'm feeling dull . . . and yes . . . bored with myself . . . kind of heavy and dragging.'
'Speak the feelings of that twelve-year-old as if you can express them now.'
'He felt . . .'
'I feel . . .'
'Yes I feel um . . . heavy and bored. This is my first year at secondary school and I'm missing the countryside and the masses of free time I'm used to having in the afternoons and I'm really sad because . . .'.

In this way heightened attention and awareness of the dullness and boredom led directly to an awareness of deep feelings of loss and loneliness. Later Gary easily recognised that his hostile dependency on Jessica was a way of avoiding experiencing his pain.

Also in this initial phase we struggled very consciously with his desire to control me, and his resentment at what he perceived to be his powerless dependency in the counselling relationship. Gary had an habitual verbal mannerism which he used to deflect the emotional impact of his experience. This involved the frequent use of the impersonal pronoun 'one' as in – 'One naturally feels bad at wanting to leave someone who loves one so much.'

I used many types of intervention to invite him into the language of responsibility. His natural curiosity and pleasure in learning (demonstrated by his choice of occupation – lecturer – and by the manner in which he had 'found' me) were strong allies in this process as I taught him about the psychology of the language of empowerment. Another type of intervention I used was the use of humour – 'Gary, if *one* feels like that, how do *two* and *three* feel about it?' This form of gentle teasing was acceptable to him since he had a well-developed sense of humour himself which he could use to amuse or to attack.

Gary's desensitisation from his own bodily processes was reflected in his increased desire to smoke whenever he felt emotional, this he showed by statements like – 'What I wouldn't give for a fag now.' Unable to smoke in my consulting room Gary directed his energy into biting his cuticles, tapping his fingers or fiddling with his shirt collar. After several sessions Gary began to realise that when he stopped agitating in these ways he became aware of an overpowering fear of being alone, which seemed to date from his infancy. Keeping Jessica around was his main method of avoidance of his primal fear, and continuing to resent her was at another level his organismic protest against the negative merging or confluence. This willingness to experience his basic fear, and to take responsibility for his dissatisfaction in his relationship with Jessica, marked the transition from him being aware of discomfort to him beginning to be in contact with the excitement and mobilisation of his resources for himself.

7

MOBILISATION AND THE POST-PRELIMINARY PHASES OF THE COUNSELLING PROCESS

An ancient saying: When not spurred, no awakening;
When not cornered, no opening through.

(Suzuki, 1972/1974: 157)

Mobilisation and Excitement

This is the stage of the counselling process when trust has begun to be established and the client has let into awareness significant aspects of his or her experience, both outside counselling and during the counselling process itself. The figure (or problem) which is most important, significant or urgent in the client's current field has been focused and clarified.

Effective work in the sensation and awareness phases makes it more possible that the client will mobilise the energy and excitement required to deal with basic issues and get his or her needs met in the present or in the future. This is therefore the next phase in the cycle of experience, or stage-post in the counselling journey.

The task of the counsellor at this stage is to facilitate the mobilisation of energies in the service of the healing process and/or to help the person to direct it. Here the way in which people use or disperse energy is most significant. Methods which are neither conducive to people getting their own needs met, nor to engaging fully in the journey of discovery which is counselling, are explored. Experiments which focus on effective and enjoyable ways of using energy are explored and validated.

At this stage clients may terminate counselling either because they feel some relief of the original pain or because they fear that further exploration may take them further than they may wish to go. For example, the wife may come to realise that if she continues to discover and assert herself as an independent self-actualising person, her husband may have less and less use for her. An investment in the marriage may effectively 'win' over an investment in her own growth needs. This is also a stage where some people may recycle the presenting problem again, for example another alcoholic binge, another ruinous affair or another wild goose chase of money-making. The results of such activities are to drain the energy away from the counselling process and to dilute the sharpness of the awareness which they gained in the first place.

Establishing a Working Alliance

The most significant part of this mobilisation phase in counselling is coming to some kind of mutual agreement or contract which two people can use to work together. In effect it is a two-way process because (at least at some level), the counsellor has to become energised, excited or interested enough in order to assume a full partnership in the endeavour. Certainly it was not unknown for Fritz Perls to fall asleep while his clients were working, and confront them in this way with the interpersonal effect of their low energy output. For myself, I do not believe that 'clients' should provide me with interest or excitement in the sense of being amusing, entertaining or interesting, yet I need to be sufficiently mobilised in order to feel engaged with them in our working alliance. When this sense of mobilisation or readiness remains absent, something is often going wrong in the counselling work.

As in almost all other cases, Gestaltists vary enormously in their approach to different situations. In Gestalt practice individual creativity always exceeds the importance of rules, prescriptions or predictions. Also, any one Gestaltist will tend to have a variety of responses from which he or she will choose those which are most accurately tuned to the requirements of the counselling moment. So, it is impossible to make rules which may very well end up being 'Gestalt introjects' of how to practise. One of the constraints of the written word which the reader has to keep in mind is that for every example used, there may be several others which could illustrate the same point but in quite a different way. Gestalt is a particular counselling approach which needs to be forged anew every moment in the uniqueness of that relationship.

Gestalt practitioners also have a tradition of being iconoclastic, extremely individualistic and even anarchic. In my opinion this was reflected in the difficulties at national and international levels of creating and maintaining training and accrediting organisations. For many people, particularly in the 1960s, accreditation, organisation and institutionalisation were dreaded. These concerns seemed inevitably associated with increasing rigidity, acceptance of authority external to the self and generally contrary to the 'I do my thing, you do your thing' philosophy of Fritz Perls (who himself was a rebellious individual who practised in some ways which would not today be considered professional or ethical). Gestalt as an approach was in fact born from the rejection of the introjects of psychoanalysis. Sometimes this has been indiscriminate and the rejection itself became *another introject* preventing development, autonomy and the enriching influence of our psychoanalytic heritage.

Another very significant part of the process at this stage is the fact that engaging in a counselling relationship often challenges the person's parental introjects. Many clients are highly protective of their parents' psychological legacies. They may try to keep from their awareness the ways in which these beloved parents neglected, abused or used them. Sometimes clients report grave conflicts with an 'inner voice' warning them not to trust this person when they are on the brink of forming a genuine working relationship. Rufus dreamed that his mother was dying and accusing him with baleful eyes of deserting her when she most needed him. In symbolic enactment he realised how scared he was of letting go of her introjected messages. He also got in touch with his love for her and his need to protect her from his growing needs for independence.

Typical Issues of the Post-preliminary (Mobilisation) Phase

Anxiety/Excitement

In this stage of the counselling process the polarity of anxiety and excitement is often highlighted. Children are frequently told: 'Don't get so excited', as if excitement in itself were damaging. What may be true is that when people get excited without direction or thoughtfulness, errors of judgement can occur. Generally the fear of excitement seems to be passed on from generation to generation, everybody seeking it and enjoying it while at the same time fearing it and attempting some internal form of control, for example, 'I mustn't get excited about this new job prospect in case it falls through.' We act as if the loss is generally 'less hurtful' if we can strip the excitement from it. If one has stripped the excitement from a project, a fantasy or an ideal, the loss hopefully will not matter. It does not hurt so much, but then neither is there commensurate joy if the project is successful.

So our culture and some parents seem bent on preventing us from getting excited as a way of protecting us from disappointment and pain. These messages become introjects which can prevent the blossoming of excitement at new potentialities – 'this counselling lark shouldn't be taken too seriously'. On the negative side parents are often phobic about the excitement in their children because of their own training in physical and emotional anaesthesia. Because children's excitement can be loud, noisy and stimulating, it can show by contrast how devoid of life and boring the grown-ups' existence has become. Karl was concerned about becoming over-excited or 'manic' in response to beautiful women, exciting music or an engrossing work project. His mother had warned him that tears would inevitably follow excitement This introjected message supported his deflection of joy, his addiction to alcohol and desensitisation to pleasurable arousal responses of all kinds.

The Gestalt approach highlights, provokes and celebrates excitement as one of the most potently creative and life-enhancing qualities of the human existence. Perls often highlighted the connection between anxiety and excitement, saying that anxiety is excitement before it has become action or 'anxiety is the gap between the *now* and the *then*. If you are in the now, you can't be anxious, because the excitement flows immediately into ongoing spontaneous activity' (Perls, 1969b: 3).

Problem Definition

Another issue at this time is the definition of the problem. Usually client and counsellor would agree about the definition of the problem. However, sometimes there can be a real discrepancy; for example, Pete defines his problem as a lack of discipline. He believes that he needs to read all the recommended books on his academic course from beginning to end in order to be a good student. He is a high achiever at university but hardly ever takes any time for relaxation or play. His parents showed approval only when he brought home prizes or awards. Neither of them valued him just for himself. People like Pete may come into counselling also hoping for 'good grades' by being 'good clients'. They have introjected messages which require obedience and performance, even when they're seeking help. This may get in the way of the clients giving energy and emotion to their basic needs (such as for play or for unconditional acceptance) which may indeed not carry the approval of their internalised parents or external authority figures.

Power Issues

A frequent arena for dispute and growth at this stage of the counselling process is the difference in experienced power between the client and the counsellor. The Gestaltist highlights the power issues and opens them for exploration and question in the ongoing work. According to Melnick and Nevis (1986) the Gestalt approach does not generate therapeutic power through disruptive or circumventive techniques. The counsellor using a Gestalt approach is employed to intervene in the lives of others (the same as any other counsellor). Here Gestalt therapy paradoxically is focused on increasing awareness of what is as opposed to helping the client change. In Gestalt the empowerment occurs through the process of the client becoming increasingly aware and interested. The Gestalt approach does not support the view that the counsellor has sole access to the truth about the client. Counsellors are willing to be questioned, confronted and challenged.

Testing the Relationship

The counselling relationship may be put to some severe testing through clients challenging the boundaries of the relationship. They may, for example, be late, miss appointments or be unwilling to do experiments. Some clients may test the relationship by withholding information such as the fact that they are seeing other practitioners (for example, a homeopath) which may affect psycho-physiological functioning in the counselling relationship as well as in their life outside.

If the counsellor is not informed of other treatments, medication or pending life changes such as bankruptcy or pregnancy, he or she will be working in a less than fully informed field, and therefore be less useful to the client. Counsellor and client also need to find ways in which they can deal with their resentments, criticisms, fears and appreciations of each other. What is important is that the counsellor be strong and authentic enough to withstand the attacks from the client and survive emotionally. As someone once said: 'the only real mistake you can make as a counsellor is to die'. (As with many statements of Gestaltists this is not meant to be a truth, but a provocation to the truth.)

Working with 'Resistance'

Resistance is a term rarely used in the Gestalt literature due to a connotation that clients will try to 'resist' or reject that which may be of benefit to them – for example, the 'truth' about their aggressive or erotic impulses. Gestalt assumes that the basic driving force of human beings is their urge to make meaning, to be curious and to develop their capacities. Therefore, given a fully capable choice, the expectation is that human beings will choose in the direction of growth and well-being and not want to 'resist' this.

It is accepted that at this moment the person can be no different from what they genuinely are. The 'interruptions to contact' (confluence, desensitisation, deflection, introjection, projection, retroflection and egotism) have in the past been called resistances to contact, perhaps as a result of our psychoanalytic legacy. Resistance or reluctance can be seen to operate only when the client has to accept a 'truth' externally imposed on him. But for many people in Gestalt, resistance (in the form of something to be overcome) is not a useful concept and contrary to the very spirit of Gestalt – appreciating the clients' subjective experiences as their phenomenological truth. What may appear as resistance is, therefore, something to be explored, understood and experienced since it is as significant a part of a person's process as any other part of his experience, and is therefore not to be labelled differentially 'bad' or 'unhelpful'. Polster and Polster (1974), in particular, stress the importance of accepting resistances, even suggesting that we drop the word because of the negative connotations that it has acquired. Use of the notion of resistance can subtly perpetuate a basic value assumption that human beings will want to reject that which can be of most value to them, and that they will need to be in adversarial relation to their putative healers.

It is probably more useful to think about the client's apparent resistance as an indication that she is defending her organismic integrity against externally imposed pressure. In this way 'resistance' in counselling could be seen as feedback that the counsellor has lost creativity and become rigid or set in a fixed Gestalt. Gestalt is based on a vision of people which expects them to welcome biological changes from within or challenges from without when they are ready to assimilate and integrate these in a mutually respectful healing relationship.

Examples of Experiments

The approaches discussed here are particularly those that may be useful in dealing with introjects. As discussed above, introjection is a very common mechanism of preventing the effective mobilisation which is necessary to progress gracefully and efficiently through the cycle.

Topdog/Underdog Dialogues

One of the most famous techniques for working with introjection is that of an enacted dialogue between the so-called topdog and underdog of a person. It can be a way of effectively dramatising the intrapsychic conflict between introjected messages, such as 'you must always work hard', and organismic needs, such as the need for play and recreation. The topdog represents that part of the personality which comments and passes judgement on the person's ongoing life, behaviour and feelings, very often in a critical and dismissive way, sometimes in ways that are quite cruel; for example 'who would want to be friends with you, you're so ugly?' The topdog also represents all introjected rules and regulations for living which we have swallowed as children and as adults. 'You shouldn't talk too much', 'you shouldn't eat like that', 'you shouldn't feel this way', etc. It is often, although not always, associated with an historical parent figure(s).

The underdog in Gestalt means that part of the personality that is apparently the victim, or the oppressed one. Sometimes it is the little-child part of the person (Finney, 1976/1983) which is harangued and beleaguered by the topdog. It is forever 'promising to do better next time' and not to drink too much, not to antagonise or not to procrastinate, as the case may be. Usually these promises turn out to be just that – promises. Like New Year's resolutions they get broken very easily and quickly. In the end the underdog usually wins in that its needs get met, albeit in a destructive way. For example, Harry resists working hard by procrastinating and delaying handing in his reports until he gets overlooked for promotion. In the meantime his topdog is kept engaged in the internal battle and Harry feels dreadful afterwards from remorse or a hangover. So a prime experimental device in Gestalt is to put these two parts of the personality in dialogue with one another. This is most usually done by the person moving from one chair (or cushion) to another and enacting the internal mental dialogue externally. Of course, this dialoguing can also be done between parts of a dream, self and a fantasised other person, or a whole cast of sub-personalities. Through the dialogue resolution, compromise, understanding or permanent divorce becomes possible.

Experiments with Eating, Chewing, Digesting and Vomiting

Experiments that focus on eating, chewing, digesting and vomiting are used to bring to awareness the ways in which clients can use introjection. Use of these techniques can help them become more aware of how they interfere with their lives in specific ways with the counselling process and with the natural and healthy unfolding of the counselling cycle.

As has been discussed earlier, Perls made major theoretical contributions to the understanding of the oral developmental phases of childhood. As a result of this there is a richness in Gestalt of techniques and experiments that have to do with all forms of 'taking in'. This may be the taking in of ideas, of values, of roles, of rules or of prejudices. At their most concrete level, people's attitudes are reflected in the way they relate to food. Whether the client 'gobbles up' anything the counsellor says, or sets his teeth and jaw stubbornly against incorporating anything from the counsellor, can seriously affect the course of the counselling relationship. If problems of this nature are not successfully addressed at the stage of establishing a working alliance, it is almost inevitable that they will recur and undermine the smooth flow of counselling at all the subsequent phases.

For the anorexic client, an experiment may involve being fed by the therapist. For a passive-aggressive person it may involve asking for feeding, taking in and valuing. For clients who swallow without tasting – chewing and masticating a piece of bread for 170 times before swallowing can bring up responses of self-consciousness, disgust and awareness of the desire to eject/avoid the problem by quickly swallowing it. Experiments such as these may bring to awareness patterns of incorporation or rejection which still curtail their lives and relationships in the present. Anyone reading this book could experiment with discovering his or her own eating behaviours by becoming aware of a process which for many of us has become either automatic or conflictful, thereby losing the potential joy and pleasure so deeply rooted at early organismic levels.

Many people have been trained in childhood to take in whatever was offered to them. They may have been rewarded for keeping within themselves toxic relationships with minimal nourishment, and prevented themselves from spitting or vomiting them out since they were the only source of nourishment they had at the time. The vomit reflex may thus be seriously impaired or decommissioned. Naturally all experiments with eating, chewing, vomiting, etc. need to be carefully calibrated to a particular client's need, and where possible should be medically monitored. For example, experiments with bulimics which may involve the counsellor supporting them during an episode of bingeing, and then remaining with them facilitating their awareness while they struggle with retaining what they have incorporated.

People with narcissistic traits have been helped by learning to account for what they have taken in from the counsellor (or from their parents) by paying attention to their eating processes, particularly remembering what they have eaten and how they have eaten with full sensory recollection.

Externalising the 'Shoulds'

Probably one of the primary tasks of becoming an autonomous self-actualising individual is to become aware of and re-examine what we have taken in as moral imperatives, what Karen Horney (1937/1977) describes as 'the tyranny of the shoulds'. Value clarification exercises can be useful and they can emerge quite naturally in the transference where the client would soon begin to articulate how the counsellor should be, for example 'warm, understanding of lateness, self-sacrificing, etc.'.

It might also be important for clients, say, to write down all the 'shoulds' that they perceive, believe in or feel persecuted by; for example, 'you should sacrifice your own needs for those of others', 'you should not be sexual', and 'you should always be a model client or a successful therapist'. In re-examining these values, people may still choose to keep some of them, but it would now be as a result of an autonomous, conscious and intentional choice related to the here-and-now reality of a person's life circumstances and not determined by the survival issues of the family of origin.

Enacting

True to its psychodramatic roots, Gestaltists often utilise the amplification of experience derived from enactment techniques. A client may be persecuted by feelings of guilt or habitually accuse herself with 'gross crimes' such as feeling unloving towards an abusive parent. For her it may be useful to become the internal judge in a dramatic and exaggerated form. This could take the form of a courtroom drama, played out in the consulting room with the client 'giving voice' to the judge's persecution, until the injustice starts to rankle. This is facilitated by techniques which invite clients to enact their drama on their introject, rather than to continue avoiding the internal accusations with shame and concealment. This externalisation of the internal persecutor enables clients to gain a new perspective and to separate 'themselves' from the tyranny of introjected values and prejudices.

Divorcing the Introjected Parent

The goal of Gestalt is an autonomous, aware and actualising person in good mutually satisfying relationship with the self, others and the environment. People who are still influenced outside of their awareness/choice by the introjected messages of their parents, schools or religions, may need (after they have become aware of their pervasive and pernicious influence on the quality of their lives) to 'divorce' the introjected parents. This procedure should not be engaged in without due clinical consideration. Premature disengagement can result in extreme feelings of abandonment and despair or provoke suicidal thoughts. Part of divorcing the parent(s) is relinquishing the hope that somehow, through being good or successful or beautiful, the parents will eventually love you properly. A certain amount of grieving is an almost inevitable consequence of this process.

Mary did this in the following sequence after more than a year in counselling. She wrote down all the resentments she felt towards her mother until she had filled a substantial exercise book and she couldn't think of any more. This was followed by a dream in which mother appeared reading this journal. In the dream Mary told her that she had no right to be doing this. She shouted at her mother: 'I won't let you control my feelings any more!'

This dream was the beginning of Mary experiencing herself as a separate and independent person who could experience all her feelings in relation to her mother. The next stage was a period of grief and sadness in truly accepting the lack of intelligent love from her mother, and a deep realisation of how her mother used her for narcissistic gratification. After this she was able to function as a separate and independent person committed to her further growth, even if it happened in directions which her mother would not have appreciated.

Enabling the Flow

As the counselling work progresses the client becomes more and more comfortable with her own energy. She is willing to enjoy arousal and excitement which is related to her biological needs and her psychological urge for growth and development. She no longer dissipates her energy because she has learned how to integrate conflicting feelings within herself. She uses this energy creatively to further her quest for self-actualisation.

Gary's Journey Continued

The excitement and mobilisation phase of the counselling relationship with Gary was established as he moved out of his confluence with Jessica and into awareness of his own real feelings in the current situation. Before he moved authentically into a working alliance with me he went through a period of testing and rebelling. For example he would try to argue with almost everything I said. By directing this mobilised energy towards the introjected part – a humiliating and verbally sadistic father, by means of experiments such as two chair dialogues, Gary allowed himself to direct his verbal aggressiveness towards the person from whom he first learnt it.

'My dad was never much of a help in the family. He was nearly always at work or talking about work.'

'Gary – imagine your dad sitting on one of the cushions in here and tell him about this.'

'You mean you want me to talk to that cushion as though it was my old man?'

'That's my suggestion.'

'And how the hell is that going to help me in the long run from feeling less scared of living alone I'd like to know?'

'Perhaps that's something else you could discuss with your father. Can you imagine him sitting over there?'

'Yea.'

'So tell him how you felt when he kept focusing on work – dad . . .'

'OK . . . well dad . . . I don't think you hardly noticed us when you got home from work. All you ever bloody did was either tell Ma all about your day at the office or you got on with some more of it at home and we weren't to disturb you.'

'Swap Gary . . . come and sit here and answer as though you are your dad responding to Gary's words.' [Swaps over to the other chair]

'Instead of bloody complaining, my son, you should be bloody grateful . . . If it wasn't for my work you'd not have had any of the nice things that you've wanted.'

Gary then moved into railing against his father for his persistent lack of support. Finally, his anger spent, he physically collapsed hugging the 'father' cushion and wept for what he'd never had.

This phase was characterised by introjection in a myriad of shapes. He was swallowing, spitting out and chewing what he took from me and his readings in Gestalt. He would become very excited about certain ideas, such as taking responsibility for yourself and rejecting control by external authorities. This was interspersed with times of global rejection of 'the system' and disgust at the 'navel-gazing' of counselling. This in turn was based on the introjection of his father's dismissive attitude towards vulnerability and self-knowledge.

I was aware of him at times seeming to want to swallow me whole, and at other times finding me and what I offered in counselling quite indigestible. This phase was punctuated by similar fluctuations in his relationship with Jessica where he experienced her as controlling him or felt guilty when he controlled her. Altogether this was a period of excitement and flux with a growing knowledge of each other and the resources at the disposal of Gary in his search for a meaningful kind of intimacy in a mature relationship.

At this point in counselling he left Jessica, not without mutual regret nor without appreciation for the important role they had played in each other's lives.

8

ACTION AND THE MIDDLE PHASES OF THE COUNSELLING PROCESS

The Zen master Yun-men said: 'In walking, just
walk. In sitting, just sit. Above all, don't wobble.'
(Watts, 1962/1974: 155)

Action – Appropriate Choice and Implementation – the Action Phase of Contact

According to Perls et al. (1951/1969: 403) this is the phase where 'there is choosing and rejecting of possibilities, aggression in approaching and overcoming obstacles, and deliberate orientation and manipulation.' This is the phase of counselling where the client has achieved motivation and mobilisation and is ready to use his energy in a purposeful action towards the satisfaction of his needs. The therapeutic relationship has been tested and found viable.

Experimenting – Approaching the Impasse

This is essentially an experimentation phase in which the client 'plays with' various options, actions, modes, roles and forms of relationship. Clients take much greater risks both in moving forward and in running away. The encouragement and facilitation of experimentation is a core value in Gestalt and the major action mode in counselling. At this stage the counsellor may invite the client to explore new possibilities of thought, feeling and behaviour. Equally the client will be experimenting with novel potentialities as natural curiosity and a willingness to take risks unfold. The emphasis is on divergent playfulness. The generation of maximum new options for the client with which to experiment, and from which eventually to choose, is now a primary activity in the counselling process.

The talent of the Gestaltist is often commensurate with the extent of his or her creative ability in the design of experiments for the client. Experiments can cover an infinite range. They can be graded in terms of difficulty for different clients at different stages of the counselling process (Nevis, in Zinker, 1978: 132–3). Always they need to be created anew from the dynamic matrix of the existential encounter. An obsessively neat person may be invited to mess up the counsellor's bookcase. A counsellor might challenge and support the client in actually telephoning her father to tell him that she loved him. Someone shy who is recalling the thrill of a child-hood circus visit might be encouraged to transform the consulting room, either in his imagination or with certain props, and to *become* the ring-master with voice, body and actions to match. For someone else who was never allowed to be critical of his parents, merely acknowledging dis-agreement with the counsellor may be a major and important experiment.

Effective experiments need to be offered at optimum moments of receptivity and initiative on the part of the client. The experienced coun-sellor will catalyse an experiment at the peak of opportunity, even though the seeds for it may have been sown months before, or in a simultaneous moment of inspired imagination. The elegant and potent experiment is usually novel, unique to the person and also a discovery for the counsellor. The second time an experiment is used it could be in danger of becoming empty 'technique' without the vibrancy, poignancy and liveliness of the creative moment of true encounter. Experiments which bring about 'good' closure of a hitherto 'poorly' closed Gestalt, are congruent with the specific issue which at that moment seems pressing for closure. There also needs to be an element of overall congruence or fit with the client's temperament, abilities and response to challenge.

One of the most important experiments in which clients might engage is that of transference. Transference is inherent in most psychotherapeu-tic relationships. Transference is 'the process by which a patient displaces on to his analyst feelings, ideas, etc., which derive from previous figures in his life' (Rycroft, 1972/1979: 168). The Gestaltist does not deny that transference in this sense occurs in the helping relationship. True to a tra-dition which emphasises inclusion, the Gestaltist may use, invite, avoid, exaggerate or minimise transference phenomena, depending on the authentic needs of the person, the timing and the training and experience of the counsellor.

The urgency of unfinished situations from the past (for example, the client's childhood) tends to be re-enacted in the present relationship with the counsellor. Experimentation in this relationship with new feelings, new attitudes and new resources leads to a fuller integration in the context of a relationship which is (with hope) less toxic and more nourishing than the original.

> The importance of new conditions in the present was perfectly understood by Freud when he spoke of the inevitable transference of the childhood fixation to the person of the analyst; but the therapeutic meaning of it is not that it is the same old story, but precisely that it is now differently worked through as a present adventure: the analyst is not the same kind of parent. And nothing is more clear, unfortunately, than that certain tensions and blocks cannot be freed unless there is a real environmental change offering new possibilities. (Perls et al., 1951/1969: 234)

Typical Issues of the Middle (Action) Phase

Transference Issues

The true essence of Gestalt is the relationship formed between counsellor and client. 'A Gestalt therapist does not use techniques; he applies *himself in* and *to* a situation with whatever professional skill and life experience he has accumulated and integrated. There are as many styles as there are therapists and clients who discover themselves and each other and together invent their relationship' (Perls, 1977: 223).

There used to be a naïve belief that Gestaltists do not work with transference. The truth of the matter is that Gestaltists work with the transference *as well as* other aspects of the relationship. The number of relational possibilities which are fostered and allowed in Gestalt between the counsellor and the client within ethical confines is diverse and varied, of which the transference relationship is but one. One of the possibilities that has been documented is the I–Thou relationship (Yontef, 1979a, 1979b, 1981, 1984, 1987; Jacobs, 1978). Another is the dialogical relationship (Hycner, 1985). Hycner differentiates the I–Thou moment or dimension from an overall dialogical approach, which encompasses the rhythmic alternation of the 'I–Thou' and 'I–It' moments (Hycner, 1985: 27).

The specific limits and boundaries are different for people with different characteristic patterns. For people with borderline personality traits it may be vital for the counsellor to be present as a real person with feelings, attitudes and history, whereas when narcissism (or egotism) is a significant feature this may be counterproductive (Tobin, 1983).

Hycner points out that a genuine dialogical relationship of full mutuality with the client is a goal of Gestalt. This real person-to-person relationship may be achieved in many different moments of the healing encounter even from the very beginning. Practically, it most frequently becomes stable in the counselling process after many intrapsychic conflicts and archaic styles of relating have been worked through. This is when the counsellor can truly become (and remain) a real person for the client.

Indeed, for most Gestaltists the genuine relationship remains the touchstone of the counselling process and all other manifestations are referred to it either later or at the time. A client was very angry with me, shouting at me and blaming me. She felt that I was deserting her for a summer vacation just at the time she most needed me. At the height of her rage, when she screamed loudly, I slowly moved closer to her and listened acceptingly to her complaint. This was the first time she had risked being so angry with me and telling me so forcefully about her needs. After the storm had passed I asked her, what would your mother do now? The question was intended to confront her projection and engage her reality testing. She replied that her mother would physically hurt or reject her. The fact that, on this emotionally charged occasion, I did neither was a breakthrough for her and for our relationship. She was now able to separate archaic expectations of destructive relationships from the benign reality of current ones.

The nature of the relationship may also change depending on different stages in the counselling process. It is often important to allow people to project onto the helping person in the beginning in order to 're-present' the original fixed Gestalt. Counsellors who refuse this opportunity to their clients may limit the potential for growth.

Countertransference Issues

Beginning counsellors are often discomforted by the idealising of them that clients do, considering them wonderful, magical, the sources of healing, comfort and wisdom. One kind of error is to hand this back to the clients and thereby too quickly deprive them of hope. There is usually plenty of time later for the client to discover the counsellor's feet of clay. Another mistake, of course, is for the counsellor to identify with the magical attributions. This leads to a consideration of countertransference.

Countertransference is usually understood to be the counsellor's 'emotional attitude toward his patient, including the response to specific items of the patient's behaviour' (Rycroft, 1972/1979: 25). Countertransference or the counsellor's emotional reactions to the client can be destructive when based on the counsellor's own unfinished business. In this way it can be the counsellor's contribution to lack of genuine here-and-now contact with a client.

However, the counsellor may also experience emotions, attitudes and impulses toward the client which are similar to those experienced by significant people from the client's past, for example the urge to reject them in the same way that a hostile parent once did. Another kind of countertransference refers to confluence (emotional merging) with the client in such a way that the counsellor experiences the feelings, attitudes or impulses which the client is experiencing (or avoiding experiencing).

It is vital for counsellors to learn to distinguish between their here-and-now reactions to the client, their reactions to the client which are based on reactions from their own past and reactions which are evoked by the client's projection onto them.

How the counsellor using the Gestalt approach will work with countertransference will vary widely from individual to individual. In any case, there are no rules, but for the purposes of this text here are some brief examples.

Bettina is recounting how her father used to beat his servants on the plantation. She is showing no feeling and telling the story as if it was a scientific report on institutionalised prejudice and the abuse of power. When I say 'You must have been so frightened for you and for them' her eyes fill with tears and she begins to own her emotional experience. My comment was prompted by a feeling of fear in the pit of my stomach which kept growing as she spoke so tonelessly about her horrific experiences.

In this instance, using my own countertransference feelings increased my contact with Bettina and helped her to be more in contact with her own experience.

In other situations the countertransference might impede effective counselling because of unresolved issues in the past of the counsellor.

Claire, an adult child of an alcoholic mother, had to work through her own unfinished business in her own personal counselling before she could become an effective counsellor for people with alcohol-related problems. Initially her own pain and confusion as a child kept intruding into her awareness as she was working with such clients, bringing tears to her eyes and preventing her from thinking clearly.

When Gregory was a little boy his mother doted on him. He became very successful in business and a 'real charmer' in social and sexual relationships. His counsellor found herself repeatedly forgetting to deal with the fact that his payment cheques to her regularly bounced. She was also reluctant to confront him with his frequent carelessness about the time of appointments, although he claimed that she was the best counsellor he had ever had and that he valued her enormously. Only in supervision, as she brought this over-protective, inappropriately nurturing response of hers to awareness, did she see how she was (in complementary countertransference) re-evoking his mother's role towards Gregory. In this process she was becoming alienated from her own realistic feelings of devaluation and depriving herself of her effectiveness as his counsellor.

Avoidance

One of Perls's central themes was the issue of avoidance. In a sense we are always avoiding something because whenever you are focusing on figure, background is being avoided, and vice-versa. At this stage of the counselling process, what has been avoided so far may become clear. For example, it may be important that the counsellor focuses John on his relationship with his father if he has primarily to date worked on his relationship with his mother. Whereas self-directed growth can be a central part of the Gestalt counselling process, the imposition of structure and therapeutic direction cannot be avoided without damage to the wholeness of the process (Melnick, 1980).

Acting-out Behaviours

At this action stage of the counselling process there is a heightened possibility of acting-out behaviour, possibly in proportion to the client's realisation that change is really possible. There is enough mobilised energy available for the organismically needed action, but the client may still choose to direct this away from completion of the instinct cycle.

Furthermore, changing might involve other changes in primary relationships such as marriage, work or choice of friends. This is a time to be alert for unplanned pregnancies, a drink-and-drive accident, sudden onset of incapacitating disease or impulsive resignation from work.

Perls frequently stressed the ambivalent nature of people's desire for health and at this stage, where people really begin to realise that transformation is possible, their courage may fail. This is a difficult phase for the counsellor because he or she may be lulled into complacency as a result of the good work already done, and not remain sufficiently alert to the threat thus posed to the client's homeostatic system.

Thinking Problems

Problems in thinking may also arise at this stage of the counselling process where action is the focus. Effective counselling work at the impasse (psychological 'stuck point') can be sustained only if it is well supported cognitively. Thinking problems such as 'thinking instead of feeling', ineffective problem-solving methods or difficulties in decision-making, must be addressed. It is sometimes necessary to teach clients very simple skills as part of being good Gestalt counsellors, when the client actually lacks those skills.

Veronica did not know how to make decisions. Long after she had dealt with the way in which her father humiliated her intelligence and her curiosity, when faced with a decision she still vacillated and dithered – whether the problem was a choice of food from a restaurant menu or a choice of husband. She needed to learn criteria for decision-making (including the use of imagination) which most people take for granted. In such ways re-education and relearning can be an important part of the counsellor's work.

Emotional Fluency

For many people a motivating reason for seeking counselling is that they experience difficulty in recognising and expressing their emotions. This may be expressed in terms such as 'I want to feel my feelings' or 'My feelings are always overwhelming me and frightening me.' In the course of counselling, people generally move away from their habitual relationship to their emotions and become more free and differentially expressive in the way that they relate emotionally with themselves and others. People's feeling lives are often handicapped and perverted by their early childhood experiences and by parental figures who may themselves have been terri-fied of feelings, or who used their emotions to abuse, persecute and manipulate others. Such alienation from the full range of our psychophys-iological emotionality is also culturally supported by norms which value a stiff upper lip or 'being cool' in the face of life-threatening events.

Chuck, a handsome and strong client who gave as his presenting problem that he was a physical coward, based this opinion of himself on the idea that he would be scared to go into battle and be under fire. Gestalt, valuing the integrity of the body/mind self, would see it as organ-ismically appropriate to be scared when your life is in danger. Denial of this survival response is not the outcome of good counselling.

Becoming in good contact with your emotions involves the whole cycle of awareness, including choosing and implementing appropriate action. There used to be an idea that true Gestaltists expressed their feelings, whether of sexual attraction or of overt hostility, in the here-and-now irre-spective of the circumstances, the people or the morality involved. I believe this was based on mistaking a stage in a process of growth for a goal of indiscriminate self-expression. For Ronald, who described himself as 'emo-tionally stunted', it was a significant stage when he, in the context of the counselling relationship and safe space, expressed whatever feeling he experienced at the time of experiencing it as strongly as he felt it. However, living in a real world, later stages of counselling might require that he learns how to contain strong feelings in certain situations such as commit-tee meetings, in order to achieve other goals which he may consider to be more important.

The person who is emotionally fluent learns to know his own feelings and be comfortable with them. He can flexibly and responsibly take or avoid the actions which are to the best benefit of himself and the people he cares about. Counsellors often find to their own dismay that they bear the brunt of a client's most frequent and most clumsy experiments because the coun-selling relationship is experienced as the safest relationship for the person.

Examples of Experiments

It is important to keep in mind that this book explores one possible pattern of conjunctions (amongst many possibilities) between phases in the Gestalt cycle and certain boundary disturbances. Derivatives of the experiments

which follow here are frequently associated with counselling work on projection.

Exercises in Brain-storming

Margery suffered from obsessively recurring worries. Hardly had she left
the house when she would begin wondering whether she had left the stove
on, or how she might get back in should she lose her key. Her use of language reflected a similar pattern; she spoke in endless circumlocutions with
innumerable qualifiers to such an extent that she was almost incompre-
hensible. Although highly intelligent, her inner experience was that she
could never give the right answer to her mother. So, when answering a
question she experienced herself as stringing together possibility after possibility after possibility, in the hope that this time she would get it right,
while 'knowing' at the same time that she never would. She projected her
mother's perfectionistic demands on any authority figure – her boss, her
counsellor, her privileged friends. Consequently she continued to communicate ineptly as if she was still a little girl 'trying to get it right'. Of
course, the harder she tried the more she failed.

For people like Margery, who project their parents' excessive demands
for perfection onto the rest of the world (thereby handicapping their own
emotional and intellectual creativity) the phase of spitting out or re-digest-
ing the introjects might need to be followed by exercises and experiments
which focus on the generation of options *without* judgement or censure,
where what is interesting or fascinating is valued more highly than what is
right or correct.

Brain-storming type exercises may take the form of sitting with a client
and his problem and encouraging him to write up as many possible solutions
as he can think of, regardless of how ridiculous or impractical they may
seem. Judgement or criticism is set aside for the duration in an atmosphere
where playful curiosity holds sway. In this way the counsellor can provide a
corrective emotional experience, challenging through the reality of the counselling relationship, the force or belief in the projection that acceptance is
always contingent on an ever-escalating demand for perfection.

Polarisation Experiments

Instead of avoiding extremes of personality, passion or propensity, Gestaltists
seek to discover, accentuate and acknowledge the widest possible differences

between people and within one particular person. Phenomenologically, Gestalt seeks not to deny difference but to bring polarisations, if not into reconciliation, then into dialogue.

Bert is a gentle, kind, self-sacrificing community worker with advanced ulcers of the stomach. Bert dedicated his life to the service of others and is still looking after his elderly mother who is completely dependent upon him. In the course of counselling, Bert gradually came to recognise and own one polarity of his persona. This was the pair which he identified as the saint and the dark vindictive, rageful, tyrannical self ('Mr Macho') whose dearest desire was to reject all the people who were so dependent on him. 'Mr Macho' wanted to live a dissolute life characterised by generally taking what he wanted because he wanted it, without any care or concern for others. In the middle phases of the counselling process he experimented with this latter, less familiar, part of himself in the counselling relationship and by drawings, two-chair work and sand-play. In this process of discovery and dialogue he was able to develop his 'macho' self and to learn from, and integrate, some of the aggressive and strong qualities into his ongoing daily life. He started to ask for what he wanted, resisted manipulation and asserted himself forcefully and clearly in situations where his needs or rights were being abrogated.

The counsellor may choose to provoke the polarisations. 'If the patient obsessively plotted every move and worried everything into existence, he was encouraged to drift. If he anxiously filled space with words, we looked for a while at wordlessness. The person who feared going down into depression permitted himself to go down and explore the going down' (Van Dusen, 1975b: 90).

Guided Fantasies

A guided fantasy is an exercise in imagination directed, evoked or encouraged by the counsellor to facilitate the client in exploring new possibilities of feeling, action and thought appropriate to novel situations. People need to begin to allow themselves to conceive of being different from the way they are. Thus a bridge is created between the current reality and the 'conceivable self'. Sometimes 'action' starts in the head. One primary way in which guided fantasy can be useful is in helping people to be in charge of recovering from illness.

Nadia was suffering from leukaemia. As part of her treatment plan the Gestalt counsellor facilitated her full bodily relaxation. He then encouraged her to visualise the armies of white blood cells fighting the cancer cells with little ray guns, and then suitably disposing of the dead cells when she went to the toilet. The image was Nadia's own, although based on pictures which were shared with her by the doctors and her counsellor. By using this technique Nadia became an active partner in her own healing process, not the victim who was 'being done to'.

Dreamwork

Dreamwork is probably one of the most commonly used ways in which counsellors believe that they are doing 'Gestalt'. This is probably because Perls was such a master at facilitating people to engage with their dream material in powerful, enlightening and transforming ways. Unfortunately, the process has also been over-used without due regard for the entire body of theory and methodology which is Gestalt. Perls did not accept the notion of the unconscious as a region of the mind which is inaccessible. Whereas Freud compared the personality to an iceberg, of which the largest portion is submerged, Perls conceived of the personality more as a rubber ball rolling and floating in water. The Gestaltist works with whichever part of the 'ball' is uppermost at any given moment, investigating its function for the client in the here-and-now.

In brief, an intervention may involve asking the dreamer to enact any one or more of the different elements of the dream. The creation, encounter and enactment of dialogue between two or more parts of the dream is based on the belief that every dream represents the whole person. Perls was of the opinion, like Jung, that every dream has an existential message for the dreamer, especially if dreamers will allow themselves to discover it freshly from within themselves and not in response to an external authority's 'interpretation'. All the elements in the dream are conceived of as being projected parts of the self which can ideally be integrated, owned or at least acknowledged. To enhance the experiential reality of feelings and symbols, dreams are told in the present tense as if the client were dreaming them now. For Freud the dream was the 'royal road to the unconscious', and for Perls it was the 'royal road to integration'.

Sharon, a twenty-four-year-old nurse, was very reluctant to engage wholeheartedly in the process of counselling because of her deep distrust of people in authority due to earlier sexual abuse by her father. She had the following dream. A baby was surrounded by a ring of fire. At first Sharon watched helplessly but then she rescued it by risking moving through the ring of fire. In the dream she then ran all the way to the counsellor's house, carrying the baby. In working with this dream she in turn became the concerned parent, the threatened baby, the ring of fire and the counsellor. She recognised in the enactment all these parts as aspects of herself. The existential message she recognised as her willingness to rescue her inner child and to trust the counsellor inside her as well as the actual counsellor.

Owning Projected Characteristics

'Owning' in the Gestalt sense means to acknowledge and take into one's awareness a particular quality or trait which already belongs to oneself. It is instructive to identify the quality that you most despise in other people. (Think of this for yourself right now.) Frequently this is a denied quality in yourself which you have projected onto other people, thus making it more comfortable to maintain the status quo within your own personality. For example, resenting racial prejudice in other people may mask acknowledgement of racial prejudice in oneself.

Projection may be positive in nature as well. Tom, who suffered from painfully low self-esteem, was invited to make up as many sentences as he could about a stone. He described the stone as 'solid', 'substantial', 'earthy', 'trustworthy', 'interesting' and 'capable of many uses'. He was then encouraged to say these qualities but prefixing them with 'I am', for example, 'I am solid', 'I am substantial', etc. As he did this experiment he realised with a shock of recognition that at least at some level he believed these complimentary things about himself. He was projecting all his positive and admirable qualities onto the stone, just as he attributed all positive and admirable qualities to his colleagues at work. It takes a good person to recognise another.

Allowing Spontaneous Growth

Enabling the counselling process to unfold spontaneously does not deprive the counsellor of potency. He or she is always there pushing, prodding, enjoying, laughing, and flowing in a sense of wonderment and fascination.

'This stance gives one the freedom to be a learner and to play with hypotheses, rather than becoming fixed in the stale truths and routine self-righteousness' (Zinker, 1978: 13).

Gary's Dream

In terms of his major interruption to contact, projection marked the middle phase of the counselling relationship with Gary. He was now eager to do experiments which led to self-discovery and had begun, to a much greater extent, to trust himself and me. During this phase he sometimes projected onto me the judgement that he wasn't being an interesting or exciting enough client for me and that I may be wanting to be with other clients or doing something else which was more interesting. He also believed that I would be frightened of his destructive rage and he felt that he wanted to protect me from it. Exercises facilitating him in owning the projected characteristics – for example saying: 'I am bored with myself. I want to be more interesting for me and I am scared of my own destructiveness' – began to take some effect.

Up to this time Gary strongly believed that his nightmares were merely the result of indigestion or over-drinking. Around this time he had the following dream, and having worked with it, changed his mind about the value of dreams:

I am driving along a dark, tree-lined road in a black stationwagon when I suddenly notice ahead of me, lying in the middle of the road, a small animal of some kind. I have trouble stopping the car and for a while am in dread that I won't be able to stop actually driving right over the poor thing. At the last moment I wrench the steering wheel to the left and skid partially off the road. The brakes now seem to be malfunctioning such that it seems as though I'll slide right down the steep edge off the road. At last a large rock blocks the car's forward plunge and with an awful jolt I come to a standstill. I get out of the car and make my way with difficulty through the undergrowth back to the road. The animal is still there and as I kneel beside it discover it to be a rather bedraggled and crippled kitten. A large blue pantechnicon then careers towards us and I seem glued to the spot, unable to get out of its deadly path.
Still dreaming – I then dream that it is the middle of the night and I'm asleep

in bed when I awaken because of an odd noise emanating from the passage outside my room. I am afraid, yet get out of bed and make my way towards the source of the noise. As I move along the dark corridor I'm suddenly caught across the neck by a piece of barbed-wire strung in front of me from wall to wall. I'm vaguely aware of an ominous presence smirking in glee at my fate as the wire decapitates me. I awaken screaming.

Gary worked with this dream on several occasions, each time gaining greater awareness and resolution. One intervention consisted in having a dialogue in the here-and-now between the bedraggled, crippled kitten and the pantechnicon. Gary, lying on the floor, enacted being the tiny, hurt kitten and while looking upwards, mewed in terror at the huge vehicle bearing down on it: 'Stop! Please stop – you'll kill me!' Having allowed himself to identify with the kitten, Gary began to own the very fearful, fragile, vulnerable part of himself which he had had to project onto the dream kitten. He allowed himself to get right into the feeling of painful terror.

This led him to re-experience several occasions where he had been in automobile accidents. These were not necessarily precipitated by him but usually occurred when he was emotionally upset and/or in a hurry. His self-destructiveness became a core issue as he identified how much one part of him wanted him dead. He recollected at this stage that his mother had had several spontaneous abortions before he was born, as well as after his birth.

In working with the second segment of the dream Gary retold the dream from the perspective of being the piece of wire:

I'm a taut, sharp and rusty piece of barbed wire and I have been nailed across the passage in Gary's home so that when he comes this way in the dark he will be garroted by me. I'm good at my job even though I have no ability to move. The evil man who brought me to the house for this purpose is hiding in the shadows waiting for the execution. There is a gentle draught in the house and as it blows past me I make a slight humming noise which awakens Gary and I hear him moving towards me. I'd like to warn him about me and the evil man but am powerless to do anything but wait for him to run into me. He comes hurrying along the passage and as he meets me I cut open the flesh of his throat and his head topples to the floor. The evil man laughs triumphantly but I see with horror the terrible destruction that I have caused and am filled with sadness and great remorse.

As the 'evil' man, Gary recounted the dream thus:

> I am a dark and evil force hiding in the guise of an ordinary man and I am intent on destroying Gary because he deserves to die. He has no right to live so I have sprung a neck trap outside his very bedroom and am now awaiting his execution. There is a whistling sound as the wind passes through the wire trap and I hear him stirring. I can hardly keep my chuckles silent as Gary hurries down the corridor and decapitates himself on my deadly wire.

At this point Gary started to sob deeply, and after I had held him for quite some time he talked about realising his identification with the destructive, evil man and his murderous anger towards his father who had abused him. By integrating the evil man and the pantechnicon (the rage and the power), as well as the vulnerable kitten and the scared person, Gary experienced great relief as well as an increased sense of wholeness. In the weeks that followed he reported a decrease in his irritability and temper outbursts with his friends and at work, and his sense of hurried anxiety was much reduced. He felt calmer and was no longer plagued by night-terrors. He also felt stronger and 'more of a man'.

Amongst the many other ways in which we worked with this dream, which was in a way the theme for this period, was to explore the polarisation between Gary's head and his body once they had been severed. This polarisation was connected for Gary to his desire for a satisfactory relationship with an equal intellectual partner and his sexual appetite which was unwilling and impatient to invest in the relationships which would be more likely to give him what he really needed. Gary and I both knew that he was well established in the counselling process, and was feeling, thinking and behaving in ways which were very different from a few months previously. His knowledge of himself was greatly enhanced. He was beginning to know how to use Gestalt in exploring his own experience inside and outside of the consulting room.

9

FINAL CONTACT AND THE LATER PHASES OF THE COUNSELLING PROCESS

MONK: How do we then attain emancipation?
MASTER: From the first we have never been in bondage, and therefore there is no need to seek release. Just use [it], just act [it] – this is indeed incomparable.

(Suzuki, 1972/1974: 98)

Final Contact – Full and Complete Contact – Resolving the Impasse

Perls et al. call this part of the whole sequence of grounds and figures *final contact*, and describe it as the 'goal of contacting' (1951/1969: 416). Temporarily the figure is so bright and vivid that there is practically no background.

Final contact is difficult to describe because it is so essentially an experience which beggars words and analysis. It might be considered similar to what Maslow (1968) called 'peak experiences'. However, it is also used to refer to experiential peaks or climaxes of grief, rage, love, insight or enlightenment. The person is often irrevocably changed as a result of such experiences.

This phase of the counselling process is characterised by spontaneity and absorption. The background or environment has been explored, perhaps cleared, and relevant concerns have changed in relation to the previous problem. In this phase we may get the acceptance and completion of the dominating unfinished situations of the client.

It is useful to consider the five layers of neuroses which Perls identified when considering the period of final contact in counselling whenever it may occur. The first layer he saw as a *cliché* layer, which represents the superficial exchanges and tokens of meaning and greeting such as a 'how do you do' handshake. The second layer, which is the *game* layer or *as-if* layer, is where we pretend to be kinder, smarter, weaker than we really feel. This is the layer of games and roles, as in 'the great doctor', 'the clinging vine', 'the self-sacrificer', 'the tough man'. When these roles are removed people experience the third layer – the *impasse*, where we experience the fear of being stuck, lost, or empty. According to Perls, most people avoid experiencing this layer of ourselves because of fear and because of our investment in continuing to avoid taking responsibility for our lives. Perls posits that every neurosis has a core which Russians call the 'sick point' and Gestaltists call 'the *impasse*' (Perls, 1975: 13).

> When approaching the existential impasse (and this does not mean minor hang-ups), the patient gets into a whirl. He becomes panic-stricken, deaf and dumb – unwilling to leave the merry-go-round of compulsive repetition. He truly feels the despair which Kierkegaard recognised as 'sickness unto death.' The existential impasse is a situation in which no environmental support is forthcoming, and the patient is, or believes himself to be, incapable of coping with life on his own. (Perls, 1975: 13)

The fourth layer is called the death layer or the *implosive* layer which appears either as death or the fear of death.

> It only appears as death because of the paralysis of opposing forces. It is a kind of catatonic paralysis: we pull ourselves together, we contract and compress ourselves, we *implode*. Once we really get in contact with this deadness of the implosive layer, then something very interesting happens. (Perls, 1969b: 56)

The later phases of counselling often focus on moving people from the impasse through the implosive layer to the next layer which is *explosion*. Through the explosions (or cathartic expressions) of genuine feelings people can begin to work through and finish situations from their past which connect with the person's authentic core or true self. These explosions may be through sobbing and crying – experiencing grief for a loss or a death which has not been assimilated. There may also be an explosion into anger with complete body involvement including shouting and even swearing. There can also be an explosion into joy or into orgasm. At their peaks these explosions (and there may be few or many of them) are the moments of final contact for the client in the counselling process. Whether dissolving into giggles or sobbing with despair, these moments are often subsequently identified as major turning points. This may be because of the emotional and physical intensity and concentrated intellectual absorption which is so characteristic of such counselling events.

Gestalt views body and psyche as a unified whole. Mere symbolic verbal expression, particularly of very early physiological trauma, is considered partial, limited and not as thorough as counselling work which includes preverbal sounds and the whole body. So, all these explosions need to be expressed through the muscles, the voice, and feelings of the person. We are psychosomatically injured and therefore in Gestalt true healing of the psychosomatic injury can come about only through a full expression of the injury at the cellular/muscular levels where the repression was originally implanted. However, these physiological and affective expressions need to be integrated with cognitive understanding and behavioural change (as in the next phase).

Throughout this phase of the contact cycle there is a coming-together of feeling, perceiving, physical and emotional aspects, in such a way that they all become foreground/figure so that one is aware of the unity of the inter-acting organism and the environment. In this phase, the impasse having been clarified and the background being cleared, the core existential issues are available for resolution. The impasses between organismic needs and their satisfaction are now figural because blocks to awareness, mobilisation and action have been clarified. This is the heart of the therapeutic work.

Typical Issues of the Later (Final Contact) Phase

'Stuckness'

The client may experience getting 'stuck' in the impasse, paralysed by fear of the unknown. In Gestalt the emphasis often is on seeking this stuck place at greatest speed, since that is certainly the place where massive energy can accumulate and where the implosion turns into explosion. This explosion may take the form of rage, grief, terror or joy. Alternatively, the person may stay in the imploded layer with greater and greater cost to the integrity of his or her true self. Clients and counsellors often experience 'getting stuck' as a negative. However, this 'stuck place' or impasse is better celebrated since the potential for change is greatest at this point where opposing forces are almost equally balanced in a state of creative tension.

For clients who tend to resolve difficulties by speedy or impulsive acts, it may be important to encourage them in holding the impasse or 'staying with the stuckness' well beyond their level of comfort. In doing this they can learn from the experience about themselves, about impasses and about the nature of an experience they have thus far avoided. This avoidance may take a passive or an active form, as discussed in the previous chapters. For the client who tends to be stuck most of the time in an indecisive and non-committed way, the greatest learning may be gained from learning to make this final contact. This may be like the trapeze artist who reported that he learnt how to jump from trapeze to trapeze by first throwing his heart over the space between and gradually learning to trust that his body would inevitably follow.

Cognitive Issues

Certain cognitive confusions, for example about the nature of personal choice, may emerge at this phase. An over-conscientious person who has been experimenting with self-assertion may resist the idea of becoming less perfectionistic, perhaps even fearing that he or she will become psychopathic. Gladys, who was originally sexually over-controlled and unresponsive, began to enjoy and celebrate her sexuality. However she went through a period where she confused this with vague desires to become a prostitute, as if the one would necessarily lead to the other.

Affective Issues

Even though some clients may have been expressing their feelings and doing affective work (such as weeping, raging, shaking or laughing) ever since the very beginning phases of the counselling process, the nature and depth of such work tends to change later in counselling. The more 'manageable' feelings become, the more people may allow themselves to experience greater intensity of feeling and deeper layers of primitive feeling than they had so far imagined. Leroy has been in counselling for some two years and has become much more familiar with his emotional life. He now allows himself to cry when his wife decides finally to leave him. For a while he feared that the depth of his feelings of grief and abandonment meant that he had regressed to the way he was before he came into counselling.

However, within a short while he realised that there was nothing pathological about his feeling this event so deeply. Rather it became a sign of his emotional health and the satisfactory establishment of an appropriate emotional response to a profound event in any person's life.

Fear of going mad, committing suicide or homicide, may arise as clients permit themselves really to plumb the depths of the feelings that they have held back for many years as they move from action to final contact. However, empty 'expression' of feelings as in people with histrionic patterns obviously needs to be clinically differentiated from a healthy emotional expressivity. Of course, repeated catharses without integration or life changes can also be empty and anti-therapeutic.

Behavioural Issues

Because the client's system is in turmoil both intrapsychically and interpersonally, this phase in the counselling is often characterised by behavioural instability. For example, Yasmina is fluctuating between her habitual compliance to her parents and culture with regard to an arranged marriage and her desire to be an autonomous person choosing for herself. The resolution may turn out to be that she chooses an arranged marriage herself for *her reasons* rather than theirs, *or* that she decides to choose her own partner in a more occidental tradition. Neither of these choices has to be made on the basis of introjected values, or on the basis of turning her own impulses against herself (retroflection). In the process of resolution, Yasmina threw tantrums, left home, changed her mind many times and generally behaved in ways which were completely uncharacteristic and atypical of her previous behavioural repertoire. Fortunately, being alert to these kinds of manifestations, her counsellor could help her creatively through this part of her process.

Learning New Skills

As people move through the impasse, they need to learn new skills in dealing with situations they have never chosen to face before, for instance, how to ask the boss for a rise, how to negotiate about sexual preferences or how to avoid visiting their parents for Christmas. I quote at some length from Erving Polster (1985: 6) as he discusses the question of whether a counsellor who was doing more teaching and instruction was still doing Gestalt:

For reasons I thought were good, what she did was spend considerable time giving her patient instructions in communicating with her friends; simple things like helping her to realize when she had not completed a sentence and so on. She was marvelously kindly in teaching her how to talk to these people. Her conversational, instructive mode is what she thought might not be Gestalt therapy. She thought it wasn't present oriented; she didn't use the empty chair to have her actually talk to her friends; she didn't ask anything about the patient's awareness. Her work did represent a faithfulness to the *contact* between her and her patient, a very sensitive contact in which she was very giving; giving exactly what she believed this particular patient, at this particular moment, needed most or was most called for by the dynamics of their interaction.

Reorientation

In this phase of counselling, people may often say something like 'This is all very well but I can't beat up a cushion at work, even though I know it helps me to feel better and think more clearly afterwards', or 'I can value having learnt to share my feelings with you, my counsellor, but I can't do it with my family or my work-mates – they would think I had gone soft.' In this phase the gulf between counselling and real life appears to be at its widest, since the client has now discovered how to use both himself and the counsellor effectively as equal partners in the healing process but as yet has a great deal to learn about the generalisation of this learning appropriately to 'life outside'.

Examples of Experiments

Retroflection is a major way (boundary disturbance) in which people can hinder themselves in the final contact phase of working with their hurts and their pains in counselling. Techniques which are focused on undoing retroflection are often very effective in helping to resolve impasses, and some of these are discussed below.

Mobilising the Muscles

A healthy person's muscles are neither cramped nor relaxed, but in a ready state for action – proactive and reactive – while maintaining a centred grounded balance. This means that whether standing, sitting, walking or lying down, the body's centre of gravity is well aligned with the ground providing support for movement or rest in a graceful, harmonious balance. To help James begin to mobilise his muscles he can be invited to lie down and allow himself to begin to experience his body. This means consciously noticing where there is tension and where there is looseness, without deliberately relaxing or deliberately tensing. 'Just move your attention throughout your body covering your head, muscles of your face, your back and chest, left and right arm, belly, buttocks, genitals and the whole of your left leg and the whole of your right leg.' Felt-awareness means a kinaesthetic appreciation from inside your body, not visualising the parts or theorising about the parts.

The client can also be invited to be aware of his breathing in order to discover how to decrease anxiety by a self-regulating attempt to correct faulty breathing during mounting excitement. Concentrated awareness of *how* she impedes full and complete breathing cycles under stress often releases the anxious person to take charge of their arousal and take responsibility for their responses and choices.

Investigating Misdirected Behaviour

When people retroflect, their behaviour is often misdirected. Sydney's self-pity and self-punishment are revealed as misdirected when he considers his answers to questions such as 'Whom do you want to pity you? Whom do you want to punish you?'

A person who retroflects is doing to herself what she did or tried to do to other persons or objects in her past. For reasons such as parental punitiveness or parental fragility, she redirects the behaviour inwards. She makes herself the target of the behaviour instead of the person or object in the environment. For example, instead of criticising her parents for their maltreatment of her, Lisa turns her criticism inward. She punishes herself by mentally berating herself for small mistakes and internally carps away at her shortcomings and inadequacies in a vicious and vindictive way. At the same time part of her still tries to please her parents as she did when she was a child by endless attempts at 'self-improvement', even though she knows that they will never really accept her. In this manner her personality is split into doer and done-to.

Gestaltists emphasise the recovery of the awareness of *how the need-fulfilling action was blocked* (allowing herself to know that she wanted to protest against her abuse), *the physical experience of doing the retroflected action* (instead of hurting herself she symbolically enacts the inhibited kicks and screams) and *the conscious awareness of how she is maintaining the retroflection in her present life* (continued inhibition of her self-protective urges by accepting without question criticism from her boss and husband). Once she understands the true original direction of her need to punish she may then be in a position to take responsibility for how she chooses to live the rest of her life.

Undoing

The treatment for retroflection is *undoing* – reversing the direction of the retroflecting act from inward (against the self) to outward. This can be done in a dramatic cathartic outburst, or gradually in stages paced to the personality and rhythm of the client over any length of time. The client often experiences such releases as cleansing, healing and liberating. As Lisa became aware of her self-abuse she experimented with fantasies and symbolic enactments of her criticising and punishing her parents for how they treated her. Undoing of the retroflections needs to be done gradually, and in stages paced to the personality and rhythm of the client over any length of time. The first step would usually be to achieve full awareness of the holding patterns in the body, the muscular inhibitions which have become rigidified into character armour or loss of spontaneity in love or aggression. In this way final contact with the true self can be experienced and re-established.

Executing the Inhibited Act

Sophie discovered in the process of counselling that her frequent respiratory diseases were the embodiment of the conflict between her wanting to rail and scream against her oppressive father whilst at the same time repressing this desire from fear of his reprisal by choking herself. These primitive and undifferentiated wishes were, so to speak, 'clenched' in her musculature. Sometimes a prematurely closed Gestalt presses for satisfaction and completion through physical action. In counselling she may be encouraged in the following way:

You can choke a pillow! Dig your fingers into it as if it were a throat. Shake it as a mastiff shakes a rat. Show it no mercy! While doing this, fiercely absorbed in

> squeezing the life out of your enemy, you will also sooner or later find yourself
> vocalizing – grunting, growling, talking, shouting. (Perls et al., 1951/1969: 175)

Sometimes people may find it silly to engage in such 'unusual' forms of expression even in the privacy of their own homes or the consulting room. *Playing* with the impasse can be the route in. Usually by executing the retroflected act the self-consciousness will change to excited spontaneity and the behaviour becomes a genuine expression of what the person had previously suppressed. Naturally, not all clients may want or need to express their feelings in this way. The skilful facilitator takes into account the person's temperament, state of readiness and preferences. It is more important to create a way to execute the inhibited act than to do it in a particular way. For Esmond, the retroflected act was making eye contact with an authority figure.

Affective Expressive Work or Catharsis

Probably at the heart of all impasse work is the undoing of retroflections by means of affective expressive work or emotional catharsis. Catharsis means, according to Aristotle, cleansing or purification – including purification of the emotions through drama or 'the purging of the effects of a pent-up emotion or repressed thoughts by bringing them to the surface of consciousness' (Macdonald, 1972: 206). In effective cathartic work the person fully and freely expresses the long-held-in feeling, often with great force and violent emotionality. Such affective work needs to be done with great care so that the person has the necessary support, both within and without, to make this growthful. Esau, having seen a film portraying the oppression of his people, was deeply distressed at the injustice. After long periods of denial, compliance or servility, Esau found a place within himself from whence he could rage on behalf of himself and on behalf of his people.

Barry Stevens (1975) describes a phenomenon which many experienced counsellors have observed. After complete psychophysiological (organismic) discharge of the kind described here there often follows shaking, trembling and involuntary body spasms. Huxley (in Stevens, 1975) corroborated this observation of the relief associated with loosening muscular and visceral 'knots'. He likened it to 'quaking' of members of the Society of Friends (Quakers). He considered it a somatic equivalent of confession and absolution in that it comprises recall of buried memories, psychophysiological abreaction and a dissipation of energy previously harmfully repressed.

Coming to Terms with the Loss of the Idealising Fantasy

It is during this phase that the client may need to accept that the fantasy he has cherished that one day the magic will happen and everything will have been different in the past, is a last hope that keeps him bound. This may involve a short or extended period of mourning for the loving parents he never had, the opportunities not taken, and the ultimate embarrassing ordinariness of the counsellor, as in *I Never Promised You a Rose Garden* (Green, 1986). Shanelle said wistfully to her counsellor: 'I have to learn how to let you still be potent for me, now that you are no longer magic.'

Bridging

In doing this work it is vital that the counsellor finds the delicate balance (which in any case may shift from moment to moment) between challenge and support. Gestalt requires that the counsellor respects the client's personal integrity. This integrity consists of the wholeness of that person, her body, her patterns of movement, her rhythms of living, her 'symptoms', her so-called 'resistances' and her vocabulary. Establishing full contact with this whole person means that the counsellor expects that at that precise moment the person represents the highest level of creative adjustment that is possible for that person at that time. No matter how dysfunctional her behaviour patterns may appear, and no matter how simple it may seem to the observer for her to relinquish for example 'self-torture', these adjustments were created as the very best possible solutions to that person's childhood dilemmas. As such they are both functional, and original works of art. It is unlikely that people will truly change unless this part of them gets heard, accepted and understood.

On the right hand of the counsellor is what Zinker calls 'revolutionary molding' (Zinker, 1978: 21). On the left hand is respect for the client's existing integrity. The challenges issued to the existing structures need to alternate with the support given to that part of the client which is eager to experience experiments and continue the growth or change process in surprising, unexpected and even more original ways.

In the creative process, the therapist enables the patient to join with him in an adventure in which the pair can constantly play all parts of this conflict drama. The therapist helps the client to be the experimenter, the teacher, the active modifier, while maintaining an attitude of understanding and respect for his client's existing stance. It is in this process of rhythmic sharing and active exploration of the client's inner life that his original personal structure begins to change. (Zinker, 1978: 22)

Gary Relives a Childhood Scene

Gary's awareness of himself and his own process had by now been well established. He found natural ways in which he could be alertly relaxed (centred) both in moments of boredom, such as sitting in traffic jams, and in times of stress, such as managing a particularly difficult faculty meeting. He had learnt to use his excitement in a goal-directed way and to mobilise his energies directly for a range of actions. It bears repeating that in every session, sometimes in every section of the session, Gary would move completely through the awareness cycle. Sometimes, however, this moving through a particular cycle would take several sessions. Focusing on the global or overall process of his counselling, at this stage we were mostly attending to the issues of final contact – full and clear experience of his need for negative confluence (destructive dependency) or re-enactment of his original pathological relationship with his mother.

One of the basic tenets of a Gestalt approach to counselling is that maturation is a continuous growth process during which a person moves from mobilising and using the support of others to effectively and satisfactorily mobilising and using his own resources, and learns to support himself in interdependent relationships with others.

Although Gary had now successfully left Jessica it soon became apparent to both of us that all his new women friends, although at first seemingly independent, soon showed tendencies to become just devoted followers of Gary rather than distinct individuals in a mutual relationship. Much of his early work had involved Gary's unfelt and unexpressed feelings towards his father. Now he gradually started focusing on his mother.

He vividly recalled and re-enacted a scene where at the age of seven he had been sent to the shops by his mother with permission to spend a small sum on himself. Here, Gary rearranged my consulting room to resemble the hall and his bedroom in his childhood home. In the hall he placed two large cushions to represent his two parents. As a young boy he relived how he, without deliberately disobeying her, had chosen a sweet that had turned out to cost a little more than the amount she had specified. On returning home she had noticed the missing pennies. He took the role of his mother, saying in a very controlled angry voice that he'd have to face the music as soon as his father returned from work. He relived the terror of the day's waiting, and screamed and shook uncontrollably on his imaginary bed.

These were the feelings which he had repressed at the time of the trauma as his actual memory of that day's waiting was of him being extremely quiet and biting his nails. But his body stored the unexpressed feelings and inhibited actions accurately for many years. This experience in the counselling setting gave him the opportunity to complete the earlier unfinished Gestalt for the first time at psychological, physiological and emotional levels. He relived hearing from his bedroom her angry and dramatic recounting of his terrible misdemeanour. This was followed by the dreaded calling of his name by his father who then, in front of his mother, bent him over and severely beat him whilst haranguing him in a booming voice about his evil dishonesty. By asking the little seven-year-old (because that is how old he seemed) gently what he was feeling and what he wanted to do I enabled Gary to move into his rage towards both his parents, especially his mother. So at this point Gary undid his retroflected fury. He used first his arms to beat both his parents, then his legs to kick out and finally he used his pelvis and his whole body to give full vent to the pent-up fury that would have been far too dangerous to show when only seven.

Deep sorrow and sadness followed as Gary allowed himself to know the depth of the betrayal that he had felt from his beloved mother. He was in a state of heightened sensitivity towards the needs of his inner child. He also went through what can only be described as a period of mourning for the love that he had hoped for from his mother, but which he had never really truly received. Intellectually he integrated his apparent need for confluence and his lingering resentment of such bonds.

Having given himself completely to the cathartic experience, Gary was helped, especially in the weeks that followed, to feel himself capable of giving himself wholeheartedly to a committed relationship. He said that he experienced his heart as having been released from a steel cage.

Certainly Gary was no longer holding back in his relationship with me, sharing his loving, angry and ambivalent feelings spontaneously as they arose.

Throughout the counselling or therapy process the major therapeutic 'tool' lies in the relationship between client and counsellor. With Gary, being very available and with him without engulfing or abandoning him, constituted the matrix of our work together.

10

SATISFACTION AND THE PENULTIMATE PHASES OF THE COUNSELLING PROCESS

A monk who came back from the mountain produced a turnip and said to the Master Gensha: 'O Master what do you say to this?' Gensha said: 'You just eat it.' 'What about the turnip that is eaten up?' asked the monk. 'You are filled, I am filled.' This was the Master's reply.

(Suzuki, 1972/1974: 44)

Satisfaction – the Experience of Satisfaction and Gestalt Completion or Post-contact

Post-contact is the aftermath of full and complete contact. It could have been annihilating or conducive to personal growth, but always some new and novel aspect of the self-environment field has been addressed and transformed. For the figure of contact filled the world with excitement, all the excitement there was; but in the aftermath it is seen to be a small change in the field (Perls et al., 1951/1969).

The analogous phase of the counselling process is characterised by the assimilation of the growth or the changes that have been made so far. Psychologically the client has passed through the cycle from sensation to awareness, to mobilisation, to action to full and final contact. She is just ready for the next phase – to start assimilating the experiences of her journey of self-discovery with satisfaction. The end-result will be that they will fade into the background and she may become unaware of them in the present. Yet they will remain part of the self in the same way that we may have forgotten what we ate yesterday, but it continues to nourish us.

Unfortunately there is a culturally based tendency to hasten towards the next figure without fully savouring the gains made. The goal of this phase in counselling is to facilitate the client in experiencing satisfaction and Gestalt completion, allowing herself to be fully and finally gratified with the contact which has occurred.

Pleasure at Completion

Both counsellor and client are faced at this point with the artist's dilemma of choosing between the Scylla of premature abandonment of the work and the Charybdis of a stultifying perfectionism. There is always more growth to be done, more realisations to be had, more skills to be learnt, more aspects of personality to be changed or shaped or validated. Unfortunately this phase of counselling is frequently rushed over, whether it be in the minutiae over a single section of a counselling session or the latter phases of a three- or five-year engagement in the counselling relationship. It is often also theoretically omitted in the Gestalt literature! Yet learning to appreciate, negotiate and punctuate our experiences at points of completion seems to be one of the most significant and profound moments of existence.

In this book I have used many case examples of apparently satisfactory conclusions to counselling moments or counselling epochs. In every counsellor's practice there are also naturally some engagements which end less successfully. A patient of Laura Perls writes:

> I am certainly not cured. In fact, I still have every symptom I ever had. I even have a new symptom I never had. I now experience some anxiety, almost unknown to me when I came to Laura. But symptoms have all been greatly reduced in intensity. And now, I feel and I'm alive. I suppose that when Lazarus came back to the world he still had the same bum leg, scraggly beard and bad breath he had before he died. But he knew that he'd been dead and now he was alive and I'm sure he knew it was a great miracle and was thankful. When I walk down the street I can see men and women and feel attracted, fearful, interested, excited. We, Laura and I, have made a miracle. I've come back to life. (Morphy, 1980: 136)

At this stage in counselling the client will now frequently come to sessions reporting successes at home and at work. Relationships outside often seem quite miraculously transformed. There is frequently some embarrassment in the form of 'I'm not sure I should still be coming.' But there are also extended periods of shared silence and deep feelings of pleasurable enjoyment of the partnership which is successfully completing the work. The counsellor's mental health and vocational productivity can be jeopardised by burnout phenomena if due respect is not granted to this phase. Counsellors *need* to spend time in the satisfaction part of the cycle for their clients' sakes, but also for their own sake.

For the client insufficient attention to this phase can result in the caricature of a 'growth-junkie' who is always 'working on another aspect of themselves' without any interleaving of periods of peace and effortless drifting. There is a lot of life which cannot be 'sorted out' by counselling, therapy, or personal work. It is important that both counsellor and client remember the prayer attributed to St Francis of Assisi: 'God, Grant me the Serenity to accept the things I cannot change, Courage to change the things I can and Wisdom to know the difference.'

Typical Issues of the Penultimate (Satisfaction) Phase

Self-consciousness

It is not unusual for clients to become rather self-conscious in this phase. It is as if they have taken on some of the language and some of the ideas of Gestalt (or another system of counselling) and wish to keep it consciously figural. They are reluctant to let the new language or new ways of working fade into oblivion as it becomes assimilated into their behavioural and affective repertoire. It is the same kind of issue as one comes across in training when people are concerned that they will 'forget it all in a couple of months'.

In my opinion anything needing to be consciously remembered over a long period of time in order not to be lost was not in the first place sufficiently well integrated. Gestalt, which becomes an habitual and natural part of one's life, is an ongoing pleasure characterised by unself-conscious smoothness and harmony, as well as the ability to have intimate relationships with people who have not been through a similar process. Excessive use of jargon (such as 'contact', 'avoidance', 'and now I am aware of', or 'you are projecting on to me'), favourite phrases from the counsellor, or once-fashionable Perlsian expressions, such as 'mind fucking', or 'elephant shit', do not suit most personalities and resemble a graft that never quite took.

The goal is more a seamless integration of what is truly characteristic of the person *and* that of Gestalt which can be fully and easily assimilated into the whole personality respecting its integrity and its style. There is no simple answer as to how this can be done. It lies in the blending of art and craft, theory and practice, personal experience and objectivity, awareness and technique, of each individual counsellor. This goal refers to the whole (Gestalt) of the counselling work which is infinitely more than the sum of its parts. Dissection of this process, as is done in books such as this one, only palely reflects the richness and value of personal experience of this approach.

Spectatoring

Spectatoring is a variant of the above kind of problem. More specifically it relates to spectatoring of the self in the sense that people are forever watching themselves in terms of 'what a good Gestaltist ought to be'. There is a sense of 'self-management' and 'roteness' about the way they manage themselves. This is, of course, not confined to Gestalt but can be observed in the clients of several different systems during the latter phases of their counselling. It seems to be part of a natural process which needs to be worked through as much as any other.

I think this can be described as the 'iatrogenic effect' of counselling in the sense that these are problems caused by the treatment itself. For the effective completion of the whole process the 'side effects of counselling' need to be monitored and cleared out through investigation of awareness, experimentation with tolerance of ambiguity and uncertainty, and confrontation where appropriate. It is possible that counsellors may not address this typical problem because of their sense that the person has now fully incorporated the system and is now able to use it effectively to work through the problems and to continue growth. Babington Smith and Farrell (1979/1980) also warn against assuming that any meaningful positive change through therapeutic intervention has occurred on the basis of clients' successfully learning the consultant's W.O.T. (or way of talking).

It is important that the counsellor understand and be alert to this possibility. She should also monitor her own investment in such an outcome through her own therapy. If this problem persists it may be necessary to return to earlier parts of the cycle and work through them more thoroughly.

Under-control or Over-control

Typically clients veer sporadically between under-control and over-control at this stage. They have learnt to be aware of their anger, for example to mobilise it and to act on it in intentional contact with the anger-provoking persons or situations. People often get angry inappropriately or excessively in outside situations, occasionally to their genuine detriment. For example, a person who used to be overly controlled and rigid may choose to lose his temper in a badly-managed job interview situation. This may be the organismically appropriate reaction, but may have too high a price. The 'organism also has a head' which may also choose to take into account the realistic long-term effects of insufficient retroflection. It becomes part of the counsellor's task to help the client to separate out what may be easy to say or enact in the counselling setting and what may be too costly elsewhere.

Over-control is less frequently a typical problem in Gestalt because as an approach it tends to focus on the development of spontaneity and expressiveness. However, there is a kind of over-control which can be manifested in interpersonal relationships especially when 'I do my thing and you do your thing', becomes separated from the organism–environment unity. It can end with one person's narcissistic controlling needs being expressed at the expense of both. This may occur when erstwhile victims turn into persecutors. They then vindictively attempt to punish partners for their share of what was in effect a mutually agreed upon pathological confluent partnership for the maintenance of which both had equal responsibility over many years. The counsellor needs to facilitate the clients in finding or discovering their own responsibility for having chosen and maintained such negative relationships without ultimately blaming themselves *or* punishing their partners. Probably the most effective avenue for learning this is the direct experience of the counsellor's own non-blaming and compassionate understanding towards the client.

'Missionary Zeal'

Another typical problem of this stage is that which can be described as missionary zeal. This quality appears in counselling when clients who have appreciated the journey appear to believe and act as if 'this is the true Bible and the one single road to salvation'. Acquaintances, friends and family often find themselves on the receiving end of what sounds like 'sales talk' for the particular counsellor or the particular approach (whether psychoanalysis, transactional analysis or Gestalt). The virtues of such a system are then extolled with an enthusiasm and faith which the counsellor concerned may find amusing, short-sighted, or even embarrassing. It appears to be a human tendency, having discovered something which really works, to want to witness and share it with others who may benefit from it or 'convert those who doubted its efficacy in the first place'. The counsellor needs to manage such a desire to share the client's 'great discovery' with respect, humility and compassion. The client probably needs to find a balance of appreciative gratitude without a feeling of obligation or compulsion to 'spread the word'. Recently qualified counsellors too can become bigoted in only valuing their own brand of training as true or important, and dismissing all other approaches without thorough investigation or curious open-mindedness.

Perfectionism

A desire to be excellent is frequently confused with the desire to be perfect. The subtle and very complex process of counselling is also vulnerable to this confusion, particularly because it is based on the assumption that people can actualise themselves. In this phase people can make unreasonable demands on themselves (and on their counsellors) always to be congruent, always healthy or always 'moving through the Gestalt cycle of awareness in the organismically appropriate way'. Carried to the extreme, even the liberating philosophy of Gestalt can become another straitjacket, when there isn't space to 'refuse to act on some desires such as the passing sexual attraction'. Sometimes clients need to be helped to reclaim the right to unfulfilled desires, the right to self-sacrifice if that is their choice or, even more simply, occasionally 'the right to feel bad' (Hazleton, 1985).

Ultimately the counsellor and the client need to come to terms with existential realities in the same way as the artist. Perhaps the product always falls short of the vision; that is the way it is. If this kind of problem is a recurrence of earlier problems of perfectionism then strategies and techniques to deal with such excessive demands (including working with childhood experiences) need to be re-done or invented. On the other hand, it seems a fact of life that human beings tend to fall short of perfection. No amount of 'counselling' can change this. The counsellor can only model a good-humoured acceptance of his or her own flaws, shortcomings and limitations. In another sense, of course, every human is already perfect – as perfectly themselves as a tree is perfectly itself.

Examples of Experiments

Since egotism can impede the satisfaction phase so profoundly, a number of techniques are presented which may assist with developing other interventions to deal with its manifestations at the corresponding later phases of the counselling process.

Focusing and Sharpening the Figure

All the earlier stages in the Gestalt cycle are in a way revisited at each stage. In order to focus and sharpen the figure in the post-contact phase it is necessary to revisit the discoveries and skills of awareness. Having discovered the self, it now becomes necessary to let go of the self, to allow the figure its fullness. Zen exercises of seeing or listening where the client allows herself to become one with the object or movement techniques, such as Tai Chi, may appear to be paradoxical but are helpful for becoming familiar with completion, post-contact and satisfaction (Franck, 1973). Becoming attuned to the cyclical rhythms of nature where seasons alternate and seeds which grow to trees eventually die again, means becoming attuned to the brightening and fading of 'figures' in our life. What seems shatteringly important today often appears to be irrelevant in a decade. Imbuing the present moment with richness, attention and concentration of the self enriches life and enhances the quality of the lived-now time and the remembering thereof.

Establishing Trust in Organismic Ebb and Flow

By this stage most clients have discovered that they can trust their own intuitive wisdom to reliably support their health and well-being.

Lynn had been taught that she needed eight hours of sleep a night by her parents and schoolteachers. For many years she accepted this, forcing herself to sleep even when she did not feel like it, and worrying about lack of sleep even though she suffered no fatigue. In fact, as is usual with people towards the end of counselling, her energy increased considerably and she appeared to need less sleep. However, she was still concerned, at some level, about the effect of this on her health. Lynn then engaged in a two-week-long experiment where she slept when it suited her and when she felt tired (within some practical limits) and whenever she felt like it. She would, for example, take ten minutes nap at tea time in the office rest room or half an hour at lunch, stay up all night with an exciting book and go to work (without any sleep in between) and then take a flexi-day with the weekend to sleep for eighteen hours or more. She experimented in this way until she had established that she could trust her need for sleep, her body's responsiveness to the demands of reality and a clear and sure recognition of sleep deprivation or satiation.

Discovering the wisdom of her sleep self-regulation was an enormous source of pride and satisfaction for her. She no longer had to count the hours of insomnia, but thoroughly enjoyed the books she could read at night when other people in the house, who had differing individual needs, were sleeping.

Appreciation of Satisfaction

Helen would often have exquisite insight and change her experience creatively but then would hasten on to the next problem of which she was aware.

After a series of sessions which involved Helen working at, and with, her mild fear of being assertive with strangers such as waiters and shop assistants, she relived a scene from her fourteenth year during which her raucous mother had embarrassed her acutely whilst returning a faulty pair of shoes belonging to Helen. Helen re-enacted the scene, stopping her mother in fantasy and explaining to her how to approach the situation more assertively and less aggressively – she even demonstrated to her mother how to do it.

This was a congruent and healing moment, but as she was leaving the session as an aside Helen said, 'Well next week I'll get on and start dealing with my dissatisfaction about work.'

The next week we did not move on. Preventing herself experiencing satisfaction and withdrawal were regular patterns in Helen's life. I suggested she imagine herself in an art gallery. The floors below were walled with sketches of the work she had completed already and the floor on which she now stood was bedecked with pictures depicting her 'fear of assertiveness' phase. I asked her to spend time wandering around this gallery enjoying, describing and absorbing them before passing on to the floors yet to come!

Giving up Over-control

These techniques specifically involve giving up egotism. Meditation or visualisation experiments which invite people into experiencing their connectedness to the universe are another Gestalt way in which to deal with the problems of over-control. Any meditation which focuses on the vast infinity of space, the incalculable infinity of time and the relative insignificance of the individual can be both challenging and healing for people who are stuck at this stage. Contrary to some of the impressions created in the 1960s, Gestalt now seeks to incorporate an awareness of the self which can only meaningfully exist within the environment. Subject can no longer be divorced from system, psyche no longer divorced from ecosystem. This systemic consciousness embraces not only trees and the ozone layers and the resources of the planet, but also our place in history and our participation in the evolving universe.

Accepting 'Good Enough'

There has been much emphasis in Gestalt about resisting, rejecting and rebelling and less emphasis on acceptance, resignation and 'letting go when good enough'. Since Gestalt seeks to amplify and celebrate polarities, as well as to facilitate integration when organismically appropriate, both of these aspects need equal emphasis in the repertoire of a well-balanced person. For those people whose habitual patterns and strengths were or became that of fighting, attack or Gestalt destruction, it may be vital to learn the more gracious arts of letting go, accepting when something is good enough and learning to define what is a 'good enough relationship', a 'good enough self-image', a 'good enough life'. Jenny had learnt how to talk openly and freely about her feelings and was expecting her friends to do the same. On a particular occasion several friends were taking leave of someone emigrating to another country. Jenny brought to the counselling session her dilemma about how far to surface the accumulated resentments and guilt which had built up with one particular friend of her friend at this farewell meeting. After discussion she decided to let sleeping feelings lie.

Stanley, looking back from the perspective of seventy-five years of his life during which he has been a marine engineer, a father, husband and lover, journalist, teacher and sportsman, blames himself for not becoming really good at any one of these because he had not achieved the outstanding honour in any of these. He fears his life has been worthless. In counselling he has to learn the true meaning of 'different horses for different courses'. He chose to come to terms with the fact that, although he did not achieve in terms of great honour in any field, he achieved a variety and wellroundedness of which he could be justifiably proud. By integrating his unique pattern through life, he makes his final meanings satisfying and profound in his twilight years.

Preparation for Ending

As we have seen, one of the primary values in Gestalt is for the person to be in contact with 'what is' – the reality of the here-and-now existence. Ideally the client will begin more and more to establish good contact with his inner world of thinking, imagination and sensation as well as with the outer environment of people, places and events. Self-defeating patterns are being replaced by self-actualising strategies. For Perls, Hefferline and Goodman awareness is still the key, since it brings into the foreground of consciousness unfinished situations which need completion. The healthy person also more and more owns his or her capacities to discover, invent or seek appropriate support. 'If he learns a technique of awareness, to follow up, to keep in contact with the shifting situation, so the interest, excitement, and growth continue, he is no longer neurotic, no matter whether his problems are "inner" or "outer"' (Perls et al., 1951/1969: 466).

Gary Continued

At this stage of treatment Gary felt so seriously about much of his new-found information and self-awareness that he became overly perfectionistic. He became self-punitive at even giving himself something as mild as a common cold. In his new relationship, which was with a very much more suitable woman, he was rather self-consciously vigilant about situations which could potentially draw him back into the destructive dependency (confluent) patterns of his past relationships. For example, he was pedantic about distinguishing between what he wanted to do and what she wanted to do. The interruption of the spontaneous process lay in his reluctance to let go of his surveillance.

It seemed as though he was, in a paradoxical way, wanting to 'manage his spontaneity' through introspection, an attempt to control the novel and the surprising, and to maintain a kind of confluence with deliberate awareness. This is another phase or aspect in which Gary needed to learn to allow himself to be abandoned again, and trusting that now he could find himself again.

In one session, as Gary was focusing on a sense of satisfaction about his 'inner journey', I suggested he enact a graduation ceremony, perhaps along the lines of those he regularly attended in his capacity as a senior lecturer. The purpose of this intervention was manifold. Firstly, it was to sharpen his awareness of what he had achieved during counselling and to provide his acknowledgement of these. It was also intended to create a preparation for eventual ending of the counselling relationship. In addition, it had a symbolic metaphorical intent – to remind him that in life, as in examinations, completion can be achieved without perfection. Finally, it was intended to introduce balance and reality so that he could more fully experience the satisfaction part of his counselling cycle, hopefully this becoming an internalised model for him to use in assessing future accomplishments. Effective and elegant therapeutic inventions usually, like good poems, carry layer upon layer of intent, intuition and meaning, only some of which are conscious and could be articulated.

Whereas he usually embarked quite spontaneously on many of the experiments I proffered, this day he thought a while and then replied: 'I think that's something I'd really enjoy and I don't want to do it today – not without due preparation. I want to spend the next week thinking about and preparing for it and I might even bring some props.' The following week Gary enacted an elaborate ceremony and roled me in ('roling in' means priming someone into a character he or she is to play; with description, mimicking posture and anything else that would 'flesh out' the personality of the person to be played) as the graduating professor. I was given a detailed certificate to present to Gary on which he had listed his many ordinary and outstanding personal and interpersonal achievements over the past few counselling years. Once I had 'capped him' he then gave a speech to the imaginary audience (the cushions), members of which were friends, Jessica, his new girlfriend and his parents.

11

WITHDRAWAL AND THE FINAL PHASES OF THE COUNSELLING PROCESS

A university professor from Tokyo came to visit a famous Zen master to attain wisdom. The Zen master invited him to a tea ceremony. The Zen master poured the tea into the professor's cup until it overflowed onto the table, but the Zen master still continued to pour. When the professor remonstrated, the Zen master likened his visitor to a full cup. He pointed out that in order to have one's cup filled it needs to first be empty.

(Reps, 1971: 17)

Withdrawal – the Organism at Rest

The final phase of the counselling process as described here is concerned with withdrawal – the process of letting go of an old Gestalt (or figure). I will remind readers again that there may be macro or micro cycles in the counselling process, and that withdrawal does not have to be the last stage. In fact there are probably smaller cycles within cycles at each of the stage-posts of the awareness cycle. Withdrawal (the organism at rest) certainly does not necessarily mean an ending. Active withdrawal can happen several times in the course of a session; for example, before commencing a new section of work. There are also times in the counselling process (such as when the counsellor goes on summer holiday) where withdrawal processes are provoked by calendar time rather than organismic time. Most changes in human lives (which may occur at any time during the period in counselling) are characterised by endings *and* beginnings.

Both client and counsellor need to become familiar with these empty spaces in their life experience, learn to tolerate them and to transform them through exploration from 'futile voids' to 'fertile voids'. This requires a willingness to stay in a state of confusion and uncertainty, as well as the responsibility for 'moving on' when the time is ripe, allowing sensation to emerge as a figure from a ground which is at the same time both empty and overflowing with possibilities and potentials.

Helping people through periods of significant transition is probably the core of the counselling process. Such transitions may involve the adjustment to a new baby, the death of a spouse, being diagnosed as terminally ill, promotion at work, a change in diet or a change in characteristic ways of relating to people, such as moving from an habitual distrusting stance to that of an open trusting attitude. The organismic process of self-regulation for most people around such transitional times or events will include a period of withdrawal.

Withdrawal in this phase of Gestalt formation and destruction means a pause and a pulling away of psychic energy from a previous preoccupation to a state of void or nothingness from which a new need/figure can emerge. In the Gestalt sense the background becomes foreground. It is very important for the counsellor to support and encourage the acceptance and exploration of the withdrawal and isolation which are a necessary part of the transition process. This needs to be balanced by an encouragement towards experimentation, concrete action and a re-establishing of connectedness with other parts of the person's life. Frequently people want to short-circuit or flee the uncomfortable process of being 'in between'. Yet the quality, attention and intentional awareness functional at this time can make the difference between whether this void or emptiness is experienced as futile or fertile.

The *emotional responses* to endings comprise at the very least anger, sorrow, frustration, helplessness, grief, depression and guilt. There are always ways in which clients can feel that they should have been better clients or that they should have remembered more of what the counsellor said, or that they shouldn't have kept 'secrets'.

> During the emotional response phase, patience, endurance and trust in the process are essential therapeutic qualities. To suppress or divert emotional reaction is a serious therapeutic error because this blocks organismic involvement. As the organismic need for emotional response changes, the therapist moves with the process and supports the process in movement. (Clark, 1982: 56)

A final aspect of the grieving process is that of *existential acceptance*. For each person this is uniquely different. It means that after the denial, the anger, the bargaining and the depression (Kübler-Ross, 1969) there follows an emotional acceptance and a cognitive integration in the matrix of our common humanity.

Endings – Terminating the Counselling Relationship

Every Gestaltist, as well as every client, will have their particular preferences for ending. Some people would rush into terminating as soon as there is some relief from pain. Some people will postpone the 'evil day' for as long as they possibly can. It is one of the least-studied phases of the counselling process and yet one of the most important, since unfinished business from the past and unfinished or avoided goodbyes will continue to interfere with full contact in any current or future goodbyes. One has to say 'goodbye' in order fully to say 'hello'.

The disintegration of an old Gestalt necessarily means the loss of a person, an attitude or an aspect of life which had been intrinsic to the previously formed Gestalt of our existence. For many clients who have had histories of unsatisfactory terminations this is a phase of great anxiety and sometimes pain. 'Grief is the emotion necessary to the process of destructuring within the Gestalt cycle. Grief is necessary to living as it is the emotional reaction to the losses we know during times of change' (Clark, 1982: 50). Gestaltists see grief as something to be experienced, fully lived, and even savoured. It is essential to life, not a problem to be overcome or even to finish.

Ideally both counsellor and client begin at approximately the same time to anticipate possible termination and, again ideally, both can give this process their full attention. Perhaps for the first time the client can allow himself or herself expression of the complete range of feelings while being helped to maintain thorough cognitive awareness of the ending of a very important relationship. This is particularly significant because so many human relationships end badly. Frequently death brings unprepared-for endings which are too abrupt, and decisions to divorce may be unilateral or too one-sided. Resignation from a job is often clouded by a myriad of extraneous features and group expectations. The therapeutic experience of satisfactory termination of the counselling relationship is therefore of exceptional *reparative* importance. Every goodbye which is well done in the present can retrospectively help heal incomplete goodbyes of the past. In addition, it is of great educative value in that it can help clients learn how better to negotiate life's many natural and unnatural endings in the future.

It is well known that every ending re-evokes previous experiences of loss and bereavement psychologically. People usually remember even childhood losses with enhanced vividness and painfulness as they negotiate adult losses. Clients also often encounter old introjects based on family taboos against the expression of sad feelings. Jemima re-contacted memories of being ridiculed for her grief at the serving-up of the family pet turkey at the Christmas feast. Even the selling of a car can restimulate the fixed Gestalts of old griefs. It is a phase characterised by great potential for avoidance – for example, 'We'll see each other again', 'I want to come into training' or 'It's not really goodbye, since I intend to see you every now and then if I need to.'

For the counsellor too this phase is problematical and often painful. It is as if you have just succeeded and begun to enjoy the fullness of this other human being in his healthy and actualising state when you have to start letting him go. Intimacy and a true mutuality of dialogue have often been established by this stage with a genuine and realistic liking and respect for each other. It is not unlike the conflicts parents experience about allowing their children to be independent. Some counsellors may cling too long, reluctant to experience the very real wrench of losing what has become a nourishing and valued relationship based on a great deal of shared history. Some counsellors, defending against their own abandonment issues, may be premature in 'kicking the little birds out of their nests so that they can fly'. It is important for counsellors to have developed sufficient self-awareness so that they can use such information about themselves effectively in service of the client.

Probably the most important factor in the successful completion of termination is the counsellor's ability to stay alive to his or her own moment-by-moment experience, intrapsychically as well as in the relationship with the client. Clients also may need to be invited, challenged or encouraged into paying exquisite attention to every possible facet and nuance of this fascinating part of the journey.

I have described here, for the purposes of this book, how some Gestaltists may deal with termination as a naturally occurring last phase of counselling which takes place over some time. Characteristically, there is a Gestalt perspective which approaches termination in a totally different way – making it a central issue from the very beginning. The individual may be asked after each session whether he or she would like to make another appointment. In this way, issues of responsibility, choice, goals of therapy and autonomy, magical attributes to the counsellor, archaic hopes, etc., can be made foci for exploration at the very start.

> A central characteristic of Gestalt therapy is that the patient as much as possi-ble carries out his own therapy, with the therapist standing by as observer–commentator and occasional guide . . . It is quite consistent with this general orientation to ask the patient as quickly as possible to take over the responsibility for deciding to continue therapy, for deciding what he is getting from it and whether he values this sufficiently to continue. (Enright, 1971: 120)

Some Gestaltists will wait for the emergence of termination issues towards the ending of the relationship, echoing the cyclic nature of experience. For some clients this may be suitable; for others not.

Typical Issues of the Final (Withdrawal) Phase

The interruption to contact which can be most characteristic of this phase is confluence. Merging and accurate empathy may be part of the healthy aspects of confluence of this stage. These may occur, for example, when the narcissistic client begins to empathise with the counsellor as a separate and independent person with different feelings and different needs from himself. However, a reluctance to withdraw from this confluence by ter-minating the counselling relationship can handicap and limit a satisfactory conclusion of the Gestalt experience cycle to withdrawal.

Reluctance or Over-eagerness to Terminate

Whatever the habitual patterns of termination were for the client in the beginning of counselling, they are likely to appear, albeit in diminished or modified form, at this phase of the process. Erstwhile impulsive people who were phobic for pain may need to be confronted by the counsellor about their over-eagerness to terminate as they again attempt to avoid it. People who masochistically protract such painful parts of their life expe-rience (docking off the dog's tail one inch at a time) may need to be precipitated into powerful and complete separation by the counsellor.

For example, one client had stayed with a previous counsellor for eleven years, making good progress. She decided to begin another counselling relationship very soon after termination with the previous counsellor. The primary task of this next counselling relationship, right from the beginning, focused on helping her to terminate within a time-limited contract.

Issues of Attachment and Separation

For most people issues of attachment, separation or withdrawal will need to be reworked again. Clients and counsellors may feel as if this had already been done. 'I feel as if I'm right back where I started.' However, they may need to re-work infantile or childhood issues of attachment and separation again. This will be at a different level of complexity, though, because they have usually developed so much in many ways since the first time they experienced the problem.

Primitive fears of abandonment, or a desire to kill off the counsellor before he has time symbolically to kill you off, are frequently activated. Imagery, dream recollection and reliving of birth processes are frequent occurrences at this stage. Gestaltists do not have a particular set of responses to this (or any other) phase. All the skill and inventiveness of the counsellor have to be brought to bear on working with these issues as each individual client meets this experience of separation in his or her unique way.

Towards the end of her counselling Ruth had a series of dreams involving train journeys to different destinations. In identifying different parts of her dream she discovered that she was also the driver of the train. As the driver she identified and incorporated into her experience of herself her feelings of competence, choice and power.

Generalisation and Integration

Although it may appear obvious to the counsellor or an outside observer, most clients need some help to generalise what they have learnt from the counselling process so they can apply it to other areas of their lives, and integrate it.

In her Gestalt counselling Janet had changed from having always to be as independent and strong as possible, to being able to ask quite easily for help, accepting it and sharing her 'soft' sides. Exploration of these two polarities within herself, through exaggeration and an enactment using masks which she had made, eventually led to an integration of these two qualities, whereas before they had been at war. The counsellor needed to help her to prepare both cognitively (through understanding) and behaviourally (through rehearsal and guided imagery) for practising some of her newly learnt behaviours with some of her outside circle of friends and some business colleagues.

Apparent 'Regression'

Many clients in the final phases of the counselling process complain that they have returned to an earlier stage of development or that they have reverted to their old symptoms. Sometimes they say 'I am worse than when I first came to see you!' In fact some recycling of issues, which the client may have resolved much earlier on, is almost inevitable towards the end. It is probably even diagnostic of the fact that they have been resolved. The client may be 'rerunning' them the same way as a person runs a tongue over a recently filled tooth several times to make sure that it has actually been done and to become acquainted with its 'new feel'.

Both client and counsellor may need to keep in mind that, although this may generally be a predictable phenomenon near the end of counselling, it is no less real or particularly unique. Amplification and exaggeration of such fears and doubts may bring them more in line with reality. It is important that each person rediscovers for himself or herself that problems resolved contain within their solutions the seeds of new problems.

> We shall not cease from exploration
> And the end of all our exploring
> Will be to arrive where we started
> And know the place for the first time.
> (Eliot, 1959/1986: 48).

Examples of Experiments

The boundary disturbance which has been paired with difficulty in the withdrawal phase for the purposes of this book is 'confluence'. As described in Chapter 4, confluence occurs when there is no appreciation of a boundary between one person and another, a sense of an object and the object sensed, a merging without discrimination of the points of difference or 'otherness' which distinguish them from each other.

Boundary Work

Boundary work was important at the beginning of the counselling process and again is very important towards the end because, whereas the client might have become over-identified or confluent with the past unfinished situation, he may now become confluent with a current one. Exercises involving disagreeing, rejecting and defining the self as different from the counsellor and other people are very important. This helps to avoid the acceptance of the counsellor's 'way of talking' (W.O.T.) which Farrell (1979/1980) warned against.

Stating personal preferences is a particular kind of boundary work for Emma, who has always had a tendency to be confluent with other people and to accept authoritative definitions of what is right, good or beautiful. She experiments through a whole period of several days where she states, if not always overtly, her preferences in all possible aspects of experience. For example, as she walks down the street she says: 'I prefer this autumn leaf to that autumn leaf, the shape of this paving stone is pleasing to me, the shape of that paving stone is not. I prefer grass to trees, and trousers to shoes,' and so on.

Like many Gestalt techniques this may seem rather simple or obvious, but it is based on a fact in perceptual psychology – people attach values to the large bulk of their perceptions. By doing this exercise Emma is not only sharpening the boundary between herself and others, but also particularly sharpening her inner sense of selfhood, underlining her right to be separate and to have preferences even about apparently trivial issues. She reports a heightened sense of self and enormous joy in taking responsibility for pre-ferring, whether or not these acts of hers are based on any criteria at all. Subsequently she starts dissolving a long-standing relationship which was dysfunctionally confluent for both people.

Rehearsal

Rehearsing potentially difficult situations before they occur may be part of building resources for clients to use once they have left counselling. Some emergencies can be planned for, others can be anticipated. Vera would be visiting her parents again for the first time in ten years. She had been badly abused as a child and made a decision in a previous counselling relation-ship to break off contact with her parents. Now, however, feeling much stronger but also curious, she is thinking of seeing them again in the light of the fact that they are growing old and may soon die. In fantasy she rehearses the scene of the meeting; also by role-playing both of her parents. She investigates in experiential depth her personal responses of fear and rage to some of the comments or actions her parents may still make which she thinks may still throw her off balance and invite her to lose her 'centre'.

Another form of rehearsal may take the form of therapeutic desensitisation to the particular issues that supported the person's low self-esteem. I sometimes refer to this as building 'psychological robustness'. For people who are good at defending themselves and 'being tough' this is not a particularly useful procedure. However, for clients who usually 'crumple' under real or imagined provocation, it may constitute a most valuable asset. The goal of counselling cannot be just learning how to cope with a presenting crisis. In my opinion it must also be improving the organism's self-regulatory processes, and this may involve learning how to stand up to possible future attacks.

John had a deep and profound sense of inferiority because of his lack of height. Any person or situation which accentuated his relative shortness in comparison with many other people caused him great embarrassment and shame. Towards the end of his counselling John had retrieved his feelings of self-worth and potency, and had established a mutually satisfactory relationship with a woman. However, he was still anxious about his ability to withstand ridicule or humiliation in moments of stress.

In a workshop the counsellor was able to set up a situation – a replay of a school playground scene. Group members gathered around (as children) saying his worst fears, shouting and teasing him, calling him 'shortie' and laughing at him. John had asked to do this work. He used the experience to reaffirm his sense of self-support through breathing, balance and groundedness, assuring himself of his ability to remain in contact with the best and strongest parts of himself even under a simulated attack.

Of course in some ways this is an artificial situation, but from the change in his physiological responses from the beginning to the end of this exercise there was no artificiality for John. He subsequently reported long-lasting and profound benefits in his confidence with other people and in his self-esteem.

Managing the Loss of the 'Old Self'

Clients often have some nostalgic fantasy about their 'old self'. In fact when this 'old self' becomes clearly separated out, and the client is no longer over-identified or confluent with that self-image, one can expect that counselling is nearing termination. However, there is often a fondness for that old part, particularly since it was forged on the anvil of very early experience in the service of survival. A highly functioning university professor who is now no longer an alcoholic and in good relation with himself, his colleagues and his work, remembers with affection how he used to mix with drunken 'down-and-outs', 'meths ladies' and 'all the lonely people'. He had come close to dying 'a romantic death' as a young man unblemished by the advancing years, mortgage worries and baldness. Clients may need to mourn this historical self-image, often in ceremonies which involve ritualistically saying thank you for the important ways in which these 'selves' served them, and perhaps weep for the loss of the innocence of that time. As someone once said, 'Counselling is a little bit like having someone spit in your soup. You can still drink the soup but now you know that it has been spat in.'

Saying Goodbye

In the course of counselling clients may have occasions to say goodbye or farewell to important people, events, or circumstances of their lives. The general principles and dynamics used for such specific pieces of work are very similar to the forces which come into play in saying goodbye to the counselling relationship itself. Often the 'good goodbye' has at least the following elements: expression and articulation of guilts, angers, fears, grief, appreciations and relief. For example, when a client identifies that there is someone who was dead with whom he has unfinished business, and to whom he wishes to say goodbye, the counsellor can proceed as follows:

> Take an empty chair, put it in front of the client and invite her to imagine the dead person sitting on it. Encourage the client to say whatever they think, feel or experience directly to the dead person. This may be resentment at not being loved enough, or guilt about not having been at their death bed. The client is then encouraged to switch chairs and take on the role of the dead person, replying to what had been said. A conversation may develop with the client switching back and forth and expressing a great deal of emotion. When the client has come to some resolution he is given a choice about whether he is ready or willing to say goodbye, the client may take responsibility for hanging on to the relationship or for terminating. Often this is accompanied by a com-

pletion of the mourning process through weeping, relief and joy. Frequently this is followed by greater energy, a disappearance of rumination and a re-establishment of interest in life and other relationships. (Tobin, 1975)

Specific techniques involve leading clients through their own specific and unique variations of this process, either week by week or repeatedly over several sessions. A client's ways of saying goodbye to the counsellor should be as many and varied as the kinds of relationship in which these two people have engaged. The most important strategic consideration is to allow the client to finish any 'unfinished business' with a counsellor in as complete a way as possible. This may require substantial periods of time to be devoted to satisfactorily preparing for withdrawal. This, perhaps more than any other, is the time to be inventive, creative, and fully respectful of the richness of that which is ending.

Some clients also like to make gifts to the counsellor at this stage – it may be a portfolio of paintings which she had made over the period of counselling, a drawing of a symbolic journey, or a simple letter of appreciation reminiscing about the good and difficult times in the relationship.

Mourning

In the final phases of counselling, as clients are preparing to take leave of the counselling relationship, they may get in touch with avoided or incomplete mourning for people in their past. This mourning work may of course also happen at other stages – indeed sometimes clients may specifically come into counselling to complete their mourning work. This indeed highlights the interwovenness of beginnings and endings in life and in Gestalt. This may be vital work to be accomplished so that loss of the counsellor does not become a displacement for the original unresolved Gestalt from the past.

In our western culture there is often a minimisation of the mourning process, in contrast to some Asian and African cultures where grieving is a ritualised expression of feelings within a community which supports the mourning individual for as long as is necessary. People are discouraged from fully reacting to their losses and a 'stiff upper lip' is admired.

Elsa's baby died shortly after birth. In her desire to take up the threads of her life as soon as possible and her reluctance to allow herself to feel the pain of this loss, Elsa immersed herself in her work and social activities with her usual efficiency. A year later she was admitted to a mental hospital with a 'nervous breakdown'.

The counsellor to whom she had been referred soon helped her to re-connect with her interrupted mourning process. He encouraged her to write letters to the baby she would have had, and to burn candles in memory of the little one. She went through a period of repeatedly sharing the hopes, lost dreams and many different feelings, from despair to relief, with close family and friends until the pain had been worked through. This enabled the completion of her mourning process and the beginning of a full recuperation.

The Fertile Void of Fore-contact: Beginning the Next Stage

> The patient comes to one because he fears the void. If he didn't fear it he would be a productive person and not need help. If the therapist also fears the void he will be unable to help the patient ... The meaning of the void and how it appears in the transference relationship must be discovered anew in each case. (Van Dusen, 1975b: 92)

Tolerating, exploring and encountering the feared empty space of the void again is usually the turning point for signalling departure. Between the satisfaction and completion of an old need and the emergence of a new need lies the experience of the void – the emptiness through which we all must pass as we let go of one set of experiences in order to fully engage with a new set of experiences.

Most myths and rituals of transformation involve some form of symbolic death and rebirth. It is signified by metaphors such as Jonah's time in the belly of the whale, Orpheus' journey to the Underworld or tribal initiation rites of isolation in dark places where time is experienced as indeterminate. This is not unlike the withdrawal which happens towards the end of any process including that of counselling, yet as long as there is life, withdrawal leads to new sensation.

> This interweaving of now and next is familiar in the individual firings of an auto engine or individual frames of movie films, each unit creating continuous motion by linking with the next. In these and other linkages, where endings and beginnings are gracefully joined, they often become undistinguishable from one another. As it is said biblically, in my end is my beginning. (Polster, 1987: 54)

Gary's Goodbye

During the final (withdrawal) phase of the counselling process with Gary he went through a period of regressed neediness and doubt about his ability to manage in the 'real world' without my weekly presence. For instance, during one session he recycled some of the introjected messages that he was a bad person and spent several days in a rather depressed state feeling that he had accomplished nothing in his counselling. At other times he felt pleased and grateful for the many things he had learned. He could clearly recognise that no matter how much hurt, fear and anger he might experience with his newly found sharpness, the joy that he was experiencing (instead of the kind of dull impatience interspersed with dramatic scenes of accident or drama) amply compensated for it.

At times Gary became nostalgic for his old self and would speak of the carefree 'character' he used to be. In an enactment exercise he took time talking to that person of the past, valuing him for what he had brought to his life and explaining that he no longer needed him.

Gary felt in touch with his organismic self, experiencing his hungers and needs waxing and waning according to his natural cycles. He felt 'disconnected' from his parents, finding that he could be with them without being enraged at his father or feeling guilty towards his mother.

Gary was also genuinely sad that his relationship with me was ending, and I felt sad too. For a while he thought of coming into training with me. In following this through with the help of guided fantasy, for example, a day in the week of a counsellor, he became aware that this was more to do with his desire to hold on to me than any real wish to take up a career which would involve substantial retraining in a helping profession as well as several years of study of Gestalt itself.

This became the last enactment of his pathological confluence played out with me. Working through the fear of being abandoned by me, the wish to reject me before I abandoned him, as well as the remnants of feeling engulfed was the bulk of the slow, careful work with Gary in this phase.

When recalling the process of his counselling Gary remembered many of the experiments described in these chapters as signposts along the way, yet emphasised that what had mattered most to him was our relationship.

When I first came to you I wanted you to change me. I was disappointed when you did not produce an easy medicine or something magical which you could just administer to me. Looking back, I was glad you didn't because otherwise I'd always be dependent on you in future times of need. What gradually became most healing for me was the consistent way in which you have been fully here for me no matter what I've chosen to explore. You have been with me yet separate throughout, in such a way that I've felt safe enough to recognise my responsibility for the outcomes and processes of my life and supported enough to rearrange some of my unfulfilling and harmful ways of things. I now can design my own magic when needed.

He brought a dream in which he travelled on an underground train and then on a cablecar up to the top of a mountain. He disembarked at the top of the mountain and looked down at the scenes below. In the valley he glimpsed me with a group of children and then picked up his knapsack and walked on.

12

RESPONSIBILITY AND FREEDOM IN COUNSELLING

When one is unenlightened, the snows of Mt. Fuji are the snows of Mt. Fuji and the water of Tassajara is the water of Tassajara.

When one seeks enlightenment, the snows of Mt. Fuji are not the snows of Mt. Fuji, and the water of Tassajara is not the water of Tassajara.

When one has attained enlightenment, the snows of Mt. Fuji are the snows of Mt. Fuji, and the water of Tassajara is the water of Tassajara.

(Fromm, 1986, p. 75)

Responsibilities of the Counsellor

The first responsibility of any counsellor is to follow the Hippocratic dictum of 'doing no harm'. As a very powerful interventionistic method capable of high-level confrontation (as well as infinite gentleness) Gestalt is certainly also capable of being abused. As with many other approaches, Gestalt has had its share of mountebanks, unethical practitioners and incompetents who have claimed to be practitioners on the flimsiest training and professional background.

It has also numbers of practitioners who uncritically introjected charismatic trainers without doing their own digestion. What has been done to Gestalt therapy was, according to Laura Perls, 'the same thing that has been done with psychoanalysis and other approaches which have become more wellknown and popular. It has become simplified and falsified and distorted and misrepresented' (Rosenfeld, 1982: 17). Gestalt is more accurately represented by several trainers and therapists in various centres of excellence, who adhere to and strive for the highest standards of competence, ethics and professionalism (Clarkson, 1988).

In the true existentialist sense the counsellor using the Gestalt approach is responsible for the authenticity of his being and behaving in the situation. There are no 'unconscious forces' to which overpowering influences can be ascribed. Counsellors using a Gestalt approach congruently are responsible for their choices, the nature and quality of their experiences, their awareness *and* their non-awareness. Gestalt counsellors are responsible for ensuring that their own dysfunctional processes do not contaminate the counselling process. To this end personal psychotherapy throughout Gestalt training is essential for Gestalt counsellors. Qualified counsellors who want to use the Gestalt approach are also advised to work with a Gestalt psychotherapist themselves (as a client) for an extended period of time before beginning to work with clients using the Gestalt approach.

Counsellors are also responsible for keeping their workload in good balance with the rest of their life, and also must be careful not to allow a wish to support others to interfere with their own self-care. Indeed, the *Code of Ethics and Practice for Counsellors* issued by the British Association for Counselling (1984: 2) states clearly:

> Counsellors, with their employers or agencies, have a responsibility to themselves and their clients and to maintain their own effectiveness, resilience and ability to help clients, and to know when their personal resources are so depleted as to make it necessary for them to seek help and/or withdraw from counselling, whether temporarily or permanently.

Counsellors of whatever persuasion are bound to respect the dignity and worth of every human being, which includes protecting the client's right to secrecy, privacy and trust by maintaining confidentiality. In so doing we create boundaries between ourselves and our clients which can rarely be perfectly maintained.

At social gatherings, conferences, in restaurants, shops, church or wherever, we may come across our clients who may be looking to us as role models of self-actualising people. But they may also be seeking to find flaws in our relationships with our family, our children, our friends in order to rationalise their own avoidances (Kottler, 1986). Gestalt is not so much an approach to counselling and psychotherapy as a way of life. Gestalt practitioners place a high value on this transparency of their lives and on role fluency, frequently welcoming challenges to their authenticity, congruity and self-awareness. Ultimately in Gestalt the counsellor's greatest responsibility is to be fully human. This is no excuse for irresponsible behaviour, but neither should it be construed as a demand for perfection.

Limitations and Resources for Self-support

As with any other approach to counselling, counsellors need to ensure that their personal therapy, training and supervision arrangements allow them to be aware of their areas of incompetency (such as the monitoring of psychotrophic drugs), as well as their areas of competence, skill and confidence. There is growing recognition that our clients are often our best supervisors, who may give us overt or covert feedback of surprising delicacy and acuity. Certainly my clients have been my most profound teachers.

Another correlate of the whole Gestalt approach is that the counsellor will always be in a process of positive development either flowing harmoniously or in a jagged, interrupted way along the cycle of awareness. Gestalt makes great demands on the counsellor in terms of personal availability, emotional spontaneity and intellectual ability. The demands can be well met only if the counsellor is well supported professionally by means of regular supervision and a peer group of colleagues. There are many qualified Gestaltists who would find it inconceivable to be practising with an active case-load and not be in some form of ongoing personal psychotherapy. It seems that this process acts as a preventative monitor for potentially damaging counsellor-induced influences, and as a source for ongoing support and challenge in the lifelong journey of self-discovery.

Personal psychotherapy also serves to keep the counsellor experientially in touch with what it means to be a client. A very experienced Gestalt counsellor friend restarted her personal therapy after several years, and she reported her surprise at the physiological realisation of how frightened and nervous she was to go for her first interview. Many years on the other side of the 'empty chair' may desensitise us to the vulnerability as well as the unusualness involved in this special kind of relationship we call counselling.

Another important resource for self-support is a satisfactory personal life which is rich in challenge, intimacy and adventure as well as in peacefulness. To be an appropriate and attractive model of Gestalt it is also desirable that counsellors be in good physical health, with the rest, recreation and diet which are suited to their own personal temperament and biological rhythms. There always seems to be something rather hypocritical about a Gestalt practitioner whose primary focus is on the integrity of the organism while coughing through a heavy cloud of cigarette smoke.

Dealing with Crises and Emergencies

Any well-trained counsellor will have had adequate experience of observing or participating in the management of severely disturbed individuals. Many individual qualified Gestaltists have professional backgrounds in mental health – for example, psychiatry, social work, clinical psychology. For individual counsellors who do not already have a comparable background in psychiatric or psychological training, specialised study of child development, psychopathology and personality theory may be required. Appropriate experience can be obtained by doing a placement (six months to a year, or longer) in a psychiatric hospital, which can lead to familiarity with psychiatric language and etiquette and being comfortable with people in psychotic states. This provides a good preparation and makes for fruitful and productive liaison with other professionals in the same field, even though a counsellor may only rarely have to deal with such states.

Training and Professional Standards in Gestalt

Some Gestalt is taught on many counselling courses in Britain, but this does not constitute a training in the Gestalt approach, or in Gestalt psychotherapy, just as those counselling courses which focus on analytic material do not train psychoanalysts! To become proficient in the Gestalt approach a counsellor will, after qualifying as a counsellor and gaining some experience of such work, engage in a process of personal psychotherapy with a Gestalt psychotherapist. Getting regular supervision of ongoing counselling work from a Gestalt supervisor would also be necessary in order to integrate the Gestalt approach into the professional work of a counsellor.

If readers would like to know more about Gestalt services, supervision and training, please contact Professor Petrūska Clarkson at PHYSIS, 12 North Common Road, London W5 2QB.

The Developmental Cycle of the Trainee Counsellor

It seems that in many cases trainee counsellors, in becoming skilful as counsellors, go through a cycle similar to the one I have been discussing throughout this book. (It is also possible that this cycle characterises the process of learning any new skill in an integrative manner – even for experienced counsellors.)

The beginning phases of learning counselling are usually marked by the need to build a sound and differentiated *sensation* function so that the counsellor can begin to be sensitive to the client as well as to the self. Beginning counsellors are often impatient with the focus on the need to listen, to reflect, to observe. Somehow this does not seem as 'valuable' as rushing in to solve problems. (However, it is characteristic of great experience in the field of therapy that psychotherapists revert to an exquisite respect for the information derived and exchanged at this level.) Beginning counsellors may need to overcome conditioned desensitisation – for example, to their own subtle responses of fear, disgust or seduction in response to the client. The next learning task is the development of *awareness*. The drawback is the blind confidence of naivety supported by massive deflections of feedback which may undermine the newfound conviction of a great new healing ability or tool – 'furor therapeuticus' (Rycroft, 1972/1979: 55).

The next phase often appears to be an increase in excitement and *mobilisation* of energy and resources leading to large-scale introjection of the system which is being studied, its language, its role models and its values. Temporarily this may be useful as a stage-post in the counsellor's development, but fixation at this stage prevents the development of an integrated and autonomous style.

The following phase can be described as beginning to choose and implement appropriate *action*, interventions or techniques within the counselling framework. Not infrequently these behaviours are based on projection of the counsellor's conflicts, attitudes and feelings onto the client. The next phase in the development of the trainee counsellor often involves an increase in confidence and competence which makes true *contact* with clients genuinely possible. Frequently this is accompanied by the learning of therapeutic abstinence (appropriate temporary retroflection) and an increase in diagnostic discrimination, selectivity of interventions and theoretical integration with practice.

The penultimate stage of *satisfaction* or post-contact is frequently seen towards the end of the training or for a year or so thereafter. The counsellor is then self-identified with the system which he or she has learnt and the counsellor 'watches' himself or herself being a good counsellor – an echo of egotism.

The last stage in this punctuation sequence is that of *withdrawal*. This phase can be hampered by an avoided or delayed confluence with the system, the approach or the particular set of conceptual tools which the trainee has so painstakingly acquired. Yet withdrawal from the whole learnt system, whether Gestalt or something else, is a necessary precondition for becoming a truly creative counsellor in your own right, with your own experience and your own intuition as your most reliable guides to integration. Of course, there is never an end or final withdrawal from this developmental cycle as long as a counsellor continues to practise. Whenever an experienced counsellor begins to assimilate new skills, new theoretical information or new depths of personal integration, he or she may begin the contact–withdrawal development cycle again.

A counsellor who has stopped growing, stopped changing or stopped risking the 'leap into the abyss of unknowing' is antithetical to the very heart of the Gestalt approach. Any theory which is not open to revision, new developments or surprising integrations is probably not suitable as a guideline for working with growing and changing human beings. At a symposium on the training of Gestalt therapists both Nevis and Smith (Brown et al., 1987) point out how even the cycle of experience (or 'the contact–withdrawal cycle' or the 'cycle of Gestalt formation and destruction') can be differently taught on different occasions to different audiences, even though there is a basic core of information which remains. Gestalt itself is in a process of evolution – on the one hand becoming more radically phenomenological; on the other hand, emphasising our psychoanalytic heritage and current connections.

Counselling as a Creative Gestalt

No matter what else I have said in this book, the core essence of Gestalt therapy and counselling lies not only in predictability of sequence or issue alone, but also in the discovery of the surprising, the novel and the unusual. Passion flows from precision. It is the marriage of the logic, rationality and science of the left hemisphere of the brain with the intuition, experiential wholeness and perceptual rhythm of the right hemi-sphere which makes great artists and great psychotherapists.

Great Gestaltists are above all artists who use structure, discipline and form in the counselling relationship, providing an exploratory space for clients to discover themselves. In this process the counsellor is also changed.

> It is out of the mutual richness of this experience, as well as the technical know-how of the therapist, that the threads of each life experience are given elegant development and substantive completion. Creative therapy is an encounter, a growth process, a problem-solving event, a special form of learning and an exploration of the full range of our aspirations for metamorphosis and ascen-dance. (Zinker, 1978: 5)

Zinker (1978: 18) even defines Gestalt therapy as the 'permission to be cre-ative'. Perls used techniques such as the 'hot seat' or dreamwork as momentary interventions to heighten the dramatic impact of learning for clients at particular moments in the context of their fluctuating relation-ship. Gestaltists are not to be recognised by technique, but by a willingness and ability to experiment and invent anew moments of creativity and fresh-ness in the interpersonal, I–Thou encounter.

This human engagement 'includes much that is ordinary: support, curiosity, kindness, bold language, laughter, cynicism, assimilation of tragedy, rage, gentleness, and toughness' (Polster, 1987: 182).

Finale

This book of ideas, cycles and procedures is offered with the hope that readers will use it to develop their own ways of discovering Gestalt.

Perls would have hated the idea of thousands of 'Gestalt clones' repro-ducing his experiments in a rote fashion, parroting his ideas of what Gestalt is. He knew that the healing process is not only an art and a craft, but also a mystery. I think he would have appreciated the following state-ment from Wittgenstein, which is in the true spirit of Gestalt:

> My propositions are elucidatory in this way: he who understands me finally rec-ognizes them as senseless, when he has climbed out through them, on them,

over them. (He must so to speak throw away the ladder after he has climbed up on it.)

He must surmount these propositions; then he sees the world rightly. Whereof one cannot speak, thereof one must be silent. (Wittgenstein, 1981/1986: 189)

13

CONCLUDING REFLECTIONS ON GESTALT'S FUTURE FRONTIERS

Gestalt therapy emerged essentially as a reaction – even a rebellion – against the prevailing scientific and psychoanalytic ethos and practice of the time. The dominant orientation at the time can variously be described as Cartesianism, Empiricism, Logical Positivism, Scientism, Modernism, The Enlightenment Project, Colonial Imperialism and so on and so forth. There are many names and nuances of names for it.

Although extensive discussions are available elsewhere, a simplified version for our purposes here would characterise this mid-twentieth century spirit of the science of psychology as committed to the belief in a knowable world. The activity of science produced knowledge of laws and general principles that could be translated into techniques for use by practitioners in specific situations. Science, and the psychologies derived from it, such as Behaviourism and Psychoanalysis were deterministic and operated on the laws of cause and effect. There is such a 'thing' as the material universe and matter is dead and inert. Life must be dissected and labelled and quantified in order to be understood.

Of course, the classical Gestaltists did not reject all these ideas in all situations, but they were *against* the hegemony of this kind of modernist ideology for human life, its healing and its growth.

Perls, Hefferline and Goodman (1951/1969) identified 4 major emphases in their work:

- to pay attention to experience, to become aware, to concentrate on the actual situation;
- to preserve the integrity, the interrelationship of socio-cultural, historical and animal/physical factors;

- to experiment; and
- to promote creativity.

They intended Gestalt to heal the splits and divisions of the person, science and psychotherapy between the following:

body	mind	to restore grace and joy
self	external world	to question the political and interpersonal threat of a science built on such an 'absurdity'
emotional (subjective)	real (objective)	to show that the 'real' is intrinsically an involvement or 'engagement'
infantile	mature	to heal the preoccupation with the past in order to adjust to an adult reality that is 'not worth adjusting to' and to esteem childhood traits which vitalise adults
biological	cultural	so that education can take over the functions of psychotherapy; and to situate us in social context, and in culture
poetry	prose	to restore the failure of communication which happens when poetry and the plastic arts become isolated and obscure
spontaneous	deliberate	to retrieve the 'unsought' and 'inspired' as a quality of all experience, not special states or individuals
personal	social	to restore community life its satisfactions, the inseparability of self and other
love	aggression	to disesteem 'a reactive passionless mildness, when only a release of aggression and willingness to destroy the old situations can restore erotic contact'
unconscious	conscious	to restore the esteem for the reality of dream, hallucination, play and art and to retreat from an overestimation of the 'reality-value' of deliberate speech, thought and introspection

Rosenblatt (1995: 47) contrasted the two currents in contemporary Gestalt as follows:

Quintessential conservative	Quintessential Fritz
routinized, rational, bureaucratic	charismatic
scholarly, proper	rebellious
structured	anarchistic
organized	chaotic
civilized	primitive
asexual, spiritual	sexual
refined	vulgar
spectator, critic, audience	creative artist
serious	playful
bourgeois, Establishment	bohemian
cognitive	intuitive
professional	personal
soothing, placating	aggressive, destructive
intellectual	visceral, gutsy
dull, flat	lively

Rosenblatt also pleads:

> The Gestalt experiment, with its emphasis on ephemeral phenomenological awareness, and the injunction for both therapist and patient to take a risk and to take responsibility, offer an opportunity to Gestalt therapists to be creative *and* connected to the lively tradition of its founders. (1995: 48)

That's all very well, but what does it *mean* for everyday life, for clinical practice, for Gestalt Psychotherapy?

What it does not mean	What it could mean
An identification with a diagnostic label: so that trainees are heard to say 'I don't know how to think about myself without my diagnostic label'	Acknowledging that the diagnostic label may contain more information about the diagnoser than the diagnosed
That more recently qualified people assess the work of novices in ways which increase a perceived distance between themselves and the less experienced practitioners	Welcoming newcomers and enacting the 'generosity of the gifted and the abundant' in sharing learning with them as well as learning from their experience
The wholesale unthinking introjection of psychoanalytic terms or procedures into Gestalt practice	The intellectual and academic work of creating or discovering terms which are idiomatically and uniquely Gestalt, from the natural Gestalt tradition, Gestalt sources and in the original Gestalt idiom

A denial of the fact that the dialogic relationship is also an experiment and the setting of a false competition between them	An acknowledgement and enactment that Gestalt is about experiment in the first place – including relationship
An elevation of the obedience to consensus-driven 'rules' – particularly in codes of ethics	Valorising the responsibility and freedom to choose – philosophical notions which used to be at the heart of Gestalt
The use of an examination system which serves the status quo and the standardisation and bureaucratisation of 'what is Gestalt'	Functioning as a rite of passage, including members who may challenge or grow or overthrow 'what their elders thought Gestalt was'
That trainees become scared and inhibited in their learning processes	Trainees celebrating their curiosity and joy in learning and unlearning for themselves
Adoption of a spurious substitute (usually from psychoanalysis) or apology for the fact that Gestalt does not have a developmental theory	An abiding appreciation for the fact that in the major canons developmental theory was seen as infantalising, reductionistic and often unnecessary and unhelpful for clients – and for trainees
The imposition of the values of a small group in defining what is or is not Gestalt without exploration, academic credibility, evidence or consultation	Instead welcoming the diversity, creativity and spontaneity of the undiscovered, the inspired, the playful and the exceptional
An ignorance or rejection of the wealth of quantitative and qualitative research efforts which have gone before and a problematising of questioning, inquiry and open-mindedness	A thorough and creditable grounding in these traditions which may involve a resocialisation out of the 'conventional paradigms' which may have been unquestioningly introjected or to which there was a reluctant submission

Other major charges are now being made against psychotherapy in general and some of these could also apply to Gestalt:

> Something in our hubristic, pathologising, Eurocentric, diagnostic, over-controlling, treatment planning, chaos-phobic, security-mongering, over-interpretive, individualistic interiority and insularity which have been divorced from our root activity of psyche-therapy has gone awry.
>
> The ideal of neutrality or non-involvement or 'not imposing your values on your client' is impossible, delusional and dangerous. The defence or rationalisation of innocent [or neutral] bystanding as 'professional behaviour' is wearing thin. (Clarkson, 1996a)

The interiority or unhealthy narcissism of psychotherapy has led to a false and destructive rupture of the inevitable and morally and ecologically necessary interconnectedness between the individual, society and the planet.

There is little doubt that childhood experiences can in many cases lead to adult disturbance. However an increasing chorus of workers in the field are beginning to question and criticise the infantilisation of clients, patients, trainees and even conference attendees.

What is seen as an unhelpful and possibly even destructive and abusive overemphasis on childhood and the unremitting use of developmental models predicated on the idiom of mother and child perpetuates a hierarchical and power based patriarchal division of knowledge and expertise.

> What is expertise? It is disciplined behavior, behavior marked by strict conformity to procedure rather than by Yankee tinkering. It is disciplined knowledge, acquired by careful attention to a carefully delimited space. It is knowledge made to order, that is, knowledge that can be reproduced by reference to its set of specifications, just as one could produce a manufactured object. It is a code of discipline, shaping the student to become someone capable of powerful emotional control; one cannot be both acting as an expert and acting wildly. It is a disciplinary instrument, knowledge made to order, that is, made for one who will order others to build bridges, pay fines, take medicine, or begin work on time. The society founded on expertise would provide the perfect example of Foucault's metaphor of 'dressage,' whereby the expert minute manipulations of the authorities result in smoothly coordinated movements in the social body performing a series of tasks. This ideal is the ideal of professionalism that was promulgated throughout the latter nineteenth century. (Hariman, 1989: 217)

Is it different now?

Gestalt as Qualitative Research in Action

I will explain why I think that Gestalt is qualitative research in action (although qualitative research is a much broader category than Gestalt). Gestalt is concerned with the quality of awareness, attention, with the integrity of experience – so is qualitative research. Because Gestalt also 'tries to lay claim to the integrity of experience itself and to fend off either its formalistic denial through abstraction and the hegemonies of social organisation and structure or its reduction into skills, techniques and tactics' (Clandinin and Connelly, 1994). Plato said that the unexamined life is not worth living. I believe the unreflected practice – whether teaching, supervision or therapy – is not worth doing either. Qualitative research concerns the examination of practice – not occasional case studies for exams or one-off researches, but constant research, all the time. Gestalt is concerned with the quality of practice, of learning, of making sense or meaning of experience – so is qualitative research. So research can be viewed as research into the qualities of experience as well as the funda-mental search for quality. Gestalt is inimical to bureaucratised order, categorisation, NVQs, credit points for agreeing with teacher or estab-lishment syllabuses – the fears of the founder rebels have come true when someone can 'fail' a 'Gestalt case study' because they did not use 'child development'.

Yet, there is no research evidence at all that these criteria facilitate better or more effective psychotherapy. In fact, the bulk of all studies show that theory has little relevance to the success of psychotherapy (Clarkson, 2001a). Why are we then concerned with Gestalt's lack of theory? Why import psychoanalytic into Gestalt when a hundred years of investigation shows up questionable outcomes, and a lack of understanding of cultural embeddedness? Gestalt is about freedom and autonomy – choices of who and where to turn to and – the invention of completely new turnings, So, what happens when diagnosis becomes the received version of 'good Gestalt'? Has anyone read what the feminist intellectuals think of *DSM IV* – and why is it not discussed? The quality of experience of those who are labelled and who do the labelling – what do we really know about that? As black people know, the ignoring or absence of an image is sometimes all that's necessary for oppression to be institutionalised. What qualities are currently being ignored or excluded from Gestalt theory, practice and supervision?

As I have shown elsewhere (Clarkson, 1993), Gestalt is one of the very few approaches which can be hospitable to the ideas of the new sciences, and indeed has always welcomed such perspectives in science and in life. In some important ways Gestalt itself emerged from a ground where they were taken seriously, not necessarily only as intellectual ideas, but as the very basis for lived experience.

After a review of the principles, values and central concerns of Gestalt it emerged that there were three major clusters of ideas around which every-thing in the primary Gestalt literature could be ordered (Clarkson, 1993) (of course, there are also other ways). Each of these three overlap and interlink with one another in an endlessly iterative way – that is, they are forever folding over and into one another, demonstrating their dynamic fractal vitality on both small, medium and large scales and over longer and shorter time periods. The three clusters are: wholeness (fractality); change (cyclicity) and relationship (connectivity). In one model of theory construction we could say they were the *foundation stones*, in another we could say they are more like the three probable virtual *orbits* which form the action and reflection trajectories of those who engage in this discipline we are calling Gestalt. I have shown (Clarkson, 1993) how these three ideas were central to the thought of Heraclitus, the presocratic father of Gestalt. I demonstrated with extensive quotations how these three ideas are centrally represented in the primary Gestalt canon (I am defining it here as works of the first generation and their sources). Then I added examples from Gestalt experiments and the findings of chaos/complexity theory and quantum physics to show how these three ideas are now at the forefront of the scientific frontiers of our time. These comparisons can be studied extensively elsewhere, here they are incredibly simplified for metaphoric and provocative purposes:

Everything is a whole (fractality)	Chaos fractal – self-similarity across scale – all parts are the whole and vice versa	Quantum principle of complementarity	Heraclitus . . . 'out of all a one and out of a one all'
Everything changes (cyclicity)	Chaotic essential unpredictability including the possible 'flipover effect' of all complex phenomena	Heisenberg's quantum principle of uncertainty. The universe is endlessly coming into being and going out of being	Heraclitus regarded the universe as a ceaselessly changing conflict of opposites, all things in a state of flux
Everything is relationship (connectivity)	The 'butterfly effect' – there is only ever relationship – but it is not necessarily causal or rational	Einstein's finding that the observer is always part of the field – 'objectivity is impossible'	Heraclitus: 'Through the oneness proper to a cycle, the one Physis manifests itself'[1]

Why are so many bright people across the world not so excited, energised and inspired by these ideas? Because these scientific discoveries are as exciting and potentially useful to humanity as the discovery of fire and more interesting than a man walking on the moon. In the words of the playwright: 'A door like this has cracked open some six times since we stood up on our hind legs. It's the best possible time to be alive, when almost everything you knew is wrong' (Stoppard, 1993: 48). Because these scientific discoveries and cultural paradigms are closer to the originating ideas, values, epistemology, ontology and methodology of classical Gestalt than the founders could have dreamt of. Because Gestalt is in danger of reverting to modernist, Newtonian, Cartesian, medical model, totalitarian controlling positivist ideas, values, epistemology, ontology and methodology. Because, more than most other articulated approaches to human pain, growth and creativity, Gestalt is compatible with, if not identical to, these scientific and cultural ideas – and I believe the future lies in this direction.

The Relational Field – Variations on I and Thou – the Role of Love in Gestalt Therapy

The willingness to engage with lived experience as whole – that means at the very least – sensing, feeling, thinking, experiencing, acting, contacting, reflecting and withdrawal of high quality.

The quality of relationship with others, with self, with world, with the corpus or body of work of one's community based on a willingness to engage wholeheartedly, intelligently, passionately. Quality relationship means not agreement with the status quo or a blandified group consensus, for example 'we Gestaltists would never suggest a feeling or an interpretation'.

Qualitative research is about a willingness to engage in dialogue with the others, the world as it dialogues back without pre-conceptions, without fear or in another set of words 'purely from the yearning curiosity of the soul as it searches for itself . . . An understanding of the ways in which any "science" or the "profession" or the "discipline" has and can become ways of enforcing compliance and obedience to the powers that be' (Denzin and Lincoln, 1994: 115).

A treasured independence born from bearing the anxieties of 'finding out for oneself' (perhaps asking a question whenever someone else makes a statement) – particularly when it appears 'self-evident' or when 'everybody' agrees with it.

A willingness to critique, both oneself and others and never to accept the validity or reliability of any observation on 'someone else's say so'. The willingness to see through 'neutrality', 'objectivity' as concepts redolent with self-deception, turning the world – and particularly people – into objects. Qualitative research has to do with subjects, subjective experience, the phenomenological quality of experience unique and inimical as it is. So is Gestalt.

The impossibility of a value-free science or a value-free therapy. The good qualitative researcher knows they are always imposing their values, as does the quality Gestalt therapist, but they are constantly searching and searching again through both the foundations and the implications of their values in every action or non-action. It cannot be made to stand still in some code of ethics. Not a hermeneutics of suspicion, but a hermeneutics of complexity – an engagement with the multi-layeredness of life.

The term **transpersonal** has a great variety of meanings, depending on which particular perspective it is meant to illuminate (Clarkson, 2001). The core of its meaning has to do with that which is more than or transcends the purely personal. It is impossible to speak of the transpersonal outside of the context of a relationship – an I-Thou – a cosmos which constitutes and reflects both macrocosmos and microcosmos.

Five Modes of Relationship in Gestalt

The nature of relationship, for the sake of psychotherapy, I have unpacked into five different modalities (Clarkson, 2003). It is important to distinguish between different forms of therapeutic relationship in Gestalt. These are:

the working alliance
the unfinished (transferential) relationship
the reparative/developmentally needed relationship
the I-Thou relationship
the transpersonal relationship.

Transpersonal

The nature of the transpersonal dimension in Gestalt therapy is difficult to describe because it is rare and because we have not yet developed an adequately nuanced language to communicate about it. For those people who find any such idea unacceptable, I have elsewhere proposed that this is the category which we reserve for inexplicable, apparently contradictory, irreducibly paradoxical and other irreal phenomena, ideas and notions. I am speaking of quantum physics and chaos and complexity theory again.

'There are more things in heaven and on earth, Horatio, than are dreamt of in your philosophy.' (Shakespeare, *Hamlet*, Act I, Scene 5) However, Jacobs wrote:

> When the full implications of Gestalt therapy are lived through, from the perspective of the I-Thou relation, then I think it is impossible to divorce transcendence – and therefore spirituality – from one's view of the nature of persons, and from the therapy process . . . and perhaps (Gestalt therapy) can re-enter the world of mutuality, with the potential and transcendence that exists when two individuals, fully responsible, allow their innermost selves to meet. (1978: 132–3)

Korn said: 'I believe that the spirit and the spiritual has been present in Gestalt therapeutic process from the beginning. Perhaps now we may affirm it and articulate some aspects with a degree of cogency and clarity' (1988: 104). Buber mentions the concept of grace as the ultimate factor which operates in the person-to-person encounter and which may make the difference between whether a patient gets better or not. '*Je le pensay, et Dieu le guarit* [we treat them, but it is God who cures them]' (Agnew, 1963: 75–7). Perls, Hefferline and Goodman (1951/1969: 248): 'natura sanat non medicus'. Indeed, Goodman's best work is entitled *Nature Heals*. 'We are in a numinous state of contact and confluence that is life-giving and healing for us both' (Korn, 1988: 101). Zinker calls this the creative process – the 'expression of the presence of God in my hands, eyes, brain, in all of me' (1978: 3).

All these quotations refer to some new thing, experience, archetypal pattern – whatever one may call it, which represents the inexpressible, the unknowable and often the intangible in the therapeutic relationship. It would be inconceivable to me to work therapeutically with any individual, group or organisation without working with how they construe, avoid, engage, transcend or manifest the kind of ephemeral eternities to which we point when we use the inadequately termed category 'transpersonal'. 'Nothing remains to me in the end but an appeal to the testimony of your own mysteries' (Buber, 1958/1984: 174). Perls, Hefferline and Goodman who were among the most vociferous spokespeople for change posited an organismic drive towards increasing wholeness and increasing perfection or goodness. 'A mechanical repetition without perfection as its aim is contrary to organic life, contrary to "creative holism"' (Smuts, 1987). That gives enormous substance to striving, to aspiration, to excellence, to becoming well.

'Given the novelty and indefinite variety of the environment, no adjustment would be possible by the conservative inherited self-regulation alone; contact must be a *creative transformation* [italics added] . . . On the other hand, creativity that is not continually destroying and assimilating an environment given in perception and resisting manipulation is useless to the organism and remains superficial and lacking in energy; it does not become deeply exciting, and it soon languishes. (Perls et al. 1951/1969: 406).

This creative transformation is individual realisation *and* collective evolution (Clarkson, 1991).

There is creative Evolution, and that real new entities have arisen in the universe, in addition to the physical conditions of the beginning. This is a universe of whole-making, not of soul-making merely . . . The view of the universe as purely spiritual, as transparent to the Spirit, fails to account for its dark opaque character ethically and rationally; for its accidental and contradictory features, its elements of error, sin and suffering, which will not be conjured away by an essentially poetic world-view . . . Holism explains both the realism and the idealism at the heart of things, and is therefore a more accurate description of reality than any of these more or less partial and one-sided world-views. (Smuts, 1987: 318)

This ability to combine real individuality with definitive relationship is one unique and important result of looking at persons quantum mechanically. Neither individuality nor relationship is lost. Neither is more primary. The question is, what is the inherent force which makes neurotic individuals want to get better, get into relationship and makes organisms evolve? Homeostasis has advantages. Self-actualisation and evolution are hard work.

For example, Physis can be seen as identical to the *élan vital* of Bergson (1965), who was such a strong influence on the early Perls.

Through the oneness proper to a cycle, the one Physis manifest itself . . . [Physis also means] to grow, to be, to become. Hence the [Physis] of a thing, is its Being, its inner dynamism, the process in which it rises up, by which it surges forth and endures, because of which it emerges as what and how it is; its upsurgence, its presencing . . . The matter at issue is the Physis of all things: their Being, their emergence, their presencing . . . Although Physis is wont to hide itself, it manifests itself in multiple ways . . . all suggest a certain oneness in multiple things, a certain *coincidentia oppositorum* (coincidence of opposites) . . . (Guerrière, 1980: 100, 102, 105)

An Aspirational Ethic

Gestalt is concerned with the good – or in the words of Zeno – for example being a good blind dog or a good bootmaker, a blind pup or a bootmaker of quality. Gestalt is concerned with learning and discovering for yourself, not introjecting the attitudes, the ideas and the pre-digested intellectual material of 'higher' status others.

Perls, Hefferline and Goodman wrote: 'Man does not strive to be good; the good is what it is human to strive for' (1951/1969: 335). In these words they are again articulating a philosophical position very similar to that of the Stoics who were grappling with this thousands of years ago in the following way:

> A good bootmaker is one who makes good boots, a good shepherd is one who keeps his sheep well, and even though good boots are in the Day-of-Judgement sense entirely worthless and fat sheep no whit better than starved sheep, yet the good bootmaker or good shepherd must do his work well or he will cease to be good.

> To be good he must perform his function . . . in performing that function there are certain things that he must 'prefer' to others, even though they are not really 'good'. He must prefer a healthy sheep or a well-made boot to their opposites . . . If a man is an artist, it is his function to produce beauty.
>
> (Murray, 1915, p. 126).

Or if one is a bootmaker – to make good boots. On the Day of Judgement it hardly matters whether you made good boots, or whether you're chic, or fat or starving. But it matters that you were doing it well. It is this that Nature, or Physis, herself works when she shapes the seed into a tree or the blind puppy into a good hound. The perfection of the tree or the blind puppy is in itself indifferent, a thing of no ultimate value. 'Yet the goodness of Nature lies in working for that perfection' (Murray, 1915: 43).

Élan vital as Physis

At the core of the Gestalt experience is the life force, the *élan vital* which has also been identified with the pre-socratic term Physis.

Now normally the *élan vital*, the life force, energizes by sensing, by listening, by scouting, by describing the world – how is the world there. Now this life force apparently first mobilizes the center – *if* you have a center. And the center of the personality is what used to be called the soul: the emotions, the feelings, the spirit. (Perls, 1969: 63–4)

Physis or Phusis is an ancient Greek word very rich in meaning. It is used to refer to life energy as it manifests in nature, in growth and healing as well as in all dimensions of creativity. Physic/physician (as in medicine) and Physics (as in quantum/chaos understandings of the world) both derive from it. Here it is used as a concept to concentrate some of the most significant qualities and aspirations of my work – in honour of everlasting change, unlearning as well as learning, living as well as dying well, the cycle as potent paradigm for human evolutionary processes, individual and culture, relationship and archetype, the importance of Nature as teacher and inspiration, the drive towards complexity, quality and wholeness, the co-existence of contradictions. Whether in individuals, couples, groups, organisations or artistic work, the central and organising theme is simply to have life – and to have it more abundantly.

I believe we are the servants of Physis, the life force or *élan vital* in psychotherapy. I believe that life force is in and through individual people and the task of psychotherapists and educators is to allow people to get back in touch with that inner force inside themselves (Clarkson, 1996b; 2002a). Thus the cycle or spiral of creative evolution continues from Heraclitus through the 'self' of Perls, Hefferline and Goodman, to the modern Gestalt of today.

The matter at issue in Heraclitus is physis . . . And correlative to the matter is a self-experience which is as deep as physis is comprehensive. The experience of physis is an experience of self for two reasons: (1) physis comprehends (encompasses) the self as it does everything else; and (2) the self is the locus where (for the human self) physis comprehends (understands) itself. Human experience is, in terms of physis, the self-experience of physis. (Guerrière, 1980: 129–30)

The striving for growth, excellence and creative adjustment is just as real for the individual and for the system of psychotherapy which we call Gestalt as for the planetary concerns which face our world today.

Being established in my life, buttressed by my thinking nature, fastened down in this transcendental field which was opened for me by my first perception, and in which all absence is merely the obverse of a presence, all silence a modality of the being of sound, I enjoy a sort of ubiquity and theoretical eternity, I feel destined to move in a flow of endless life, neither the beginning nor the end of which I can experience in thought, since it is my living self who think of them, and since thus my life always forestalls and survives itself . . . At the level of being it will never be intelligible that the subject should be both *naturans* and *naturatus,* infinite and finite. But if we rediscover time beneath the subject, and if we relate to the paradox of time those of the body, the world, the thing, and other people, we shall understand that beyond these, there is nothing to understand. (Merleau-Ponty, 1962: 36–5)

Note

1   In a personal communication from Professor Gerard Naddaf (25 August 1995) he wrote, '*Phusis* is, in my view, the single most important concept in ancient philosophy. Indeed, it is the centrepiece of Western philosophy . . . What you say on Heraclitus could very well have come from my own pen.'

Further Reading

Clarkson, P. (1989a) 'Responsibility and Freedom in Gestalt', *Self and Society* 17(7): 36–41.

Clarkson, P. (1989b) 'Variations on I and Thou', Keynote speech at British Gestalt Conference.

Clarkson, P. (1991a) 'Individuality and Commonality in Gestalt', *British Gestalt Journal*, 1(1): 28–37.

Clarkson, P. (1991b) Gestalt Therapy is Changing: Part I – From the Past to the Present, *British Gestalt Journal*, 1(2): 87–93.

Clarkson, P. (1993a) 'Two Thousand Five Hundred Years of Gestalt – From Heraclitus to the Big Bang', *British Gestalt Journal* 2(1): 4–9.

Clarkson, P. (1993b) *On Psychotherapy*. London: Whurr.

Clarkson, P. and Mackewn, J. (1993c) *Fritz Perls*. London: Sage.

Clarkson, P. (1995) *Change in Organisations*. London: Whurr.

Clarkson, P. (1996) 'Researching the "Therapeutic Relationship" in Psychoanalysis, Counselling and Psychotherapy: A Qualitative Inquiry', *Counselling Psychology Quarterly*, 9(2): 143–62

Clarkson, P. (1997a) Gestalt Therapy is Changing: Part II – From the Present to the Future, *British Gestalt Journal* 6(1): 29–39.

Clarkson, P. (1997b) 'Variations on I and Thou', *Gestalt Review* 1(1): 56–70.

Clarkson, P. (1997c) 'The Beginning of Gestalt', *Gestalt Journal* 20(2): 23–42.

Clarkson, P. (2002) 'Beyond Schoolism', pp. 1–14 in P. Clarkson, *On Psychotherapy 2: Including the Seven-Level Model*. London: Whurr.

References

Agnew p. 63 in E. Berne (1966), *Principles of Group Treatment*. New York: Grove Press.

Babington Smith, B. and B.A. Farrell (eds) (1979/1980) *Training in Small Groups: A Study of Five Methods*. Oxford: Pergamon Press.

Bergson, H. (1965) *Creative Evolution*. London: Macmillan.

Berne, E. (1970) Book review in *American Journal of Psychiatry*, 126(10): 163–4.

Binswanger, L. (1958) 'The Existential Analysis School of Thought', in R. May, E. Angel and H.F. Ellenberger (eds), *Existence – A New Dimension in Psychiatry and Psychology*. New York: Clarion Books.

Bowlby, J. (1953) 'Some Pathological Processes set in Motion by Early Mother–Child Separation', *Journal of Mental Science*, 99: 265.

Bridges, W. (1980/1984) *Transitions: Making Sense of Life's Changes*. Reading, MA: Addison Wesley.

Briggs, J. and Peat, F.D. (1990) *Turbulent Mirror: An Illustrated Guide to Chaos Theory and Science of Wholeness*. New York: Harper & Row.

British Association for Counselling (1984) *Code of Ethics and Practice for Counsellors*, Form No. 14. Rugby: British Association for Counselling.

Brown, G., R. Harman, E. Mintz, S.M. Nevis and E.W.L. Smith (1987) 'The Training of Gestalt Therapists: A Symposium', *Gestalt Journal*, 10(2): 73–106.

Buber, M. (1958/1984) *I and Thou*. Edinburgh: T. and T. Clark (first published 1937, second edition first published 1958).

Burchfield, R.W. (ed.) (1976) *A Supplement to the Oxford English Dictionary*. Oxford: Oxford University Press.

Cannon, W.B. (1932) *Wisdom of the Body*. New York: Norton.

Capra, F. (1976/1978) *The Tao of Physics*. London: Fontana (first published 1975).

Clandinin, D.J. and Connelly, F.M. (1994) 'Personal Experience Methods', pp. 413–27 in N.K. Denzin and Y.S. Lincoln (eds), *Handbook of Qualitative Research*. London: Sage.

Clark, A. (1982) 'Grief and Gestalt Therapy', *Gestalt Journal*, 5(1): 49–63.

Clarkson, P. (1975) 'Seven-Level Model'. Invitational chapter delivered at the University of Pretoria, November.

Clarkson, P. (1988) 'Gestalt Therapy – An Up-date', *Self and Society*, 16(2): 74–9.

Clarkson, P. (1989) 'Jungian Gestalt – Conceptual Convergence and Experiential Divergence', Jungian Gestalt Workshop, London.

Clarkson, P. (1991) 'Individuality and commonality in Gestalt', *British Gestalt Journal* 1(1): 28–37.

Clarkson, P. (1993) 'Two Thousand Five Hundred Years of Gestalt: From Heraclitus to the Big Bang', *British Gestalt Journal*, 2(1): 4–9.

Clarkson, P. (1996a) *The Bystander: An End to Innocence in Human Relationships?* London: Whurr.

Clarkson, P. (1996b) 'The Archetype of Physis: The Soul of Nature – Our Nature', *Harvest: Journal for Jungian Studies*, 42(1): 70–93.

Clarkson, P. (1997) 'The Beginning of Gestalt', *Gestalt Journal* 20(2): 23–42.

Clarkson, P. (2001a) 'Beyond schoolism', pp. 1–14 in P. Clarkson, *On Psychotherapy 2*. London: Whurr.

Clarkson, P. (2001b) *The Transpersonal Relationship in Psychotherapy*. London: Whurr.

Clarkson, P. (2002a) 'The Clarkson Seven-Level Model: Developing Epistemological Consciousness about Psychotherapy', pp. 146–72 in P. Clarkson, *On Psychotherapy 2: Including the Seven-Level Model*. London: Whurr.

Clarkson, P. (2002b) 'Physis: A Psychophilosophical Life Science Study of Autopoiesis in Psychoanalysis, Jungian Psychology and Other Psychotherapies'. Available from www.nospine.com

Clarkson, P. (2003) *The Therapeutic Relationship*, 2nd edn. London: Whurr.

Conduit, E. (1987) 'Davanloo in Britain', *Changes*, 5(2): 333–7.

Delisle, G. (1988) *Balises II: A Gestalt Perspective of Personality Disorders*. Montreal: Le Centre d'Intervention Gestaltiste, Le Reflet.

Denzin, N.K. and Lincoln, Y.S. (eds) (1994) *Handbook of Qualitative Research*. London: Sage.

Dublin, J.E. (1977) 'Gestalt Therapy, Existential–Gestalt Therapy and/Versus "Perls-ism"', pp. 124–50 in E.W. Smith (ed.), *The Growing Edge of Gestalt Therapy*. Secaucus, NJ: Citadel Press.

Eliot, T.S. (1959/1986) *Four Quartets*. London: Faber and Faber (first published 1944).

Enright, J.B. (1971) 'An Introduction to Gestalt Techniques', pp. 107–24 in J. Fagan and I.L. Shepherd (eds), *Gestalt Therapy Now*. New York: Harper and Row (first published 1970).

Fagan, J. (1977) 'The Gestalt Approach as "Right Lobe" Therapy', pp. 58–68 in E.W. Smith (ed.), *The Growing Edge of Gestalt Therapy*. Secaucus, NJ: Citadel Press.

Farrell, B.A. (1979/1980) 'Work in Small Groups: Some Philosophical Considerations', pp. 103–15 in B. Babington Smith and B.A. Farrell (eds), *Training in Small Groups: A Study of Five Methods*. Oxford: Pergamon Press.

Finney, B.C. (1976/1983) 'Let the Little Child Talk', pp. 385–419 in C. Hatcher and P. Himelstein (eds), *The Handbook of Gestalt Therapy*. New York: Jason Aronson.

Franck, F. (1973) *The Zen of Seeing*. New York: Vintage Books.

Frankl, V.E. (1964/1969) *Man's Search for Meaning*. London: Hodder and Stoughton (first published 1959, revised edition first published 1962).

Freud, S. (1955) *The Interpretation of Dreams*. New York: Basic Books (first published 1900).

Friedlaender, S. (1918) *Schöpferische Indifferenz*. München: Georg Muller.

Fromm, E. (1986) *Psychoanalysis and Zen Buddhism*. London: Unwin Paperbacks (first published 1960).

Gagnon, J.H. (1981) 'Gestalt Therapy with the Schizophrenic Patient', *Gestalt Journal*, 4(1): 29–46.

Goldstein, K. (1939) *The Organism*, Book 6. New York: America Books.

Goodman, P. (1977) *Nature Heals: The Psychological Essays of Paul Goodman*. Highland, NY: The Gestalt Journal.

Green, H. (1986) *I Never Promised You a Rose Garden*. London: Hodder and Stoughton (first published 1964).

Guerrière, D. (1980) 'Physis, Sophia, Psyche', pp. 86–134 in J. Sallis and K. Maly (eds), *Heraclitean Fragments: A Companion Volume to the Heidegger/Fink Seminar on Heraclitus*. Huntsville, AL: University of Alabama Press.

Hall, R.A. (1977) 'A Schema of the Gestalt Concept of the Organismic Flow and its Disturbance', pp. 53–7 in E.W. Smith (ed.), *The Growing Edge of Gestalt Therapy*. Secaucus, NJ: Citadel Press.

Hariman, R. (1989) 'The Rhetoric of Inquiry and the Professional Scholar', pp. 211–32 in H.W. Simons (ed.), *Rhetoric in the Human Sciences*. London: Sage.

Hazleton, L. (1985) *The Right to Feel Bad*. New York: Ballantine Books.

Horney, K. (1937/1977) *The Neurotic Personality of Our Time*. London: Routledge and Kegan Paul.

Husserl, E. (1970) *The Crisis of European Sciences and Transcendental Phenomenology*. Evanston, IL: Northwestern University Press (first published 1936).

Hycner, R.H. (1985) 'Dialogical Gestalt Therapy: An Initial Proposal', *Gestalt Journal*, 8(1): 23–49.

Jacobs, L. (1978) 'I–Thou Relation in Gestalt Therapy'. Unpublished doctoral dissertation. Los Angeles, CA: California School of Professional Psychology.

Kahn, C.H. (1981) *The Art and Thought of Heraclitus: An Edition of the Fragments with Translation and Commentary*. Cambridge: Cambridge University Press.

Koffka, K. (1935) *Principles of Gestalt Psychology*. New York: Harcourt, Brace and World.

Köhler, W. (1947/1970) *Gestalt Psychology: An Introduction to New Concepts in Modern Psychology*. New York: Liveright.

Kottler, J.A. (1986) *On Being a Therapist*. San Francisco: Jossey-Bass.

Kübler-Ross, E. (1969) *On Death and Dying*. New York: Macmillan.

Lee, M.A., O.G. Cameron and J.F. Gredon (1985) 'Anxiety and Caffeine Consumption in People with Anxiety Disorders', *Psychiatry Research*, 15(2): 211–17.

Lewin, K. (1952) *Field Theory in Social Science: Selected Theoretical Papers*. London: Tavistock Publications (first published 1951).

Macdonald, A.M. (ed.) (1972) *Chambers Twentieth Century Dictionary*. London: W. and R. Chambers.

Maslow, A. (1968) *Toward a Psychology of Being*. New York: Van Nostrand.

Masterson, J.F. (1976) *Psychotherapy of the Borderline Adult: A Developmental Approach*. New York: Brunner/Mazel.

Melnick, J. (1980) 'The Use of Therapist-imposed Structure in Gestalt Therapy', *Gestalt Journal*, 3(2): 4–20.

Melnick, J. and S.M. Nevis (1986) 'Power, Choice and Surprise', *Gestalt Journal*, 9(2): 43–51.

Merleau-Ponty, M. (1962) *The Phenomenology of Perception* (trans. by C. Smith). London: Routledge and Kegan Paul.

Merleau-Ponty, M. (1973) 'Phenomenology and the Sciences of Man', pp. 47–105 in M. Natanson (ed.), *Phenomenology and the Social Sciences*. Evanston, IL: Northwestern University Press.

Moreno, Z. (1979) 'Escape Me Never', *Group Psychotherapy, Psychodrama and Sociometry*, 32: 5–12.

Morphy, R. (1980) 'An Inner View of Obsessional Neurosis', *Gestalt Journal*, 3(1): 120–36.

Murray, G. (1915) *The Stoic Philosophy*. London: Watts, Allen & Unwin.

Naranjo, C. (1982) 'Gestalt Conference Talk 1981', *Gestalt Journal*, 5(1): 3–19.

Onions, C.T. (ed.) (1973) *The Shorter Oxford English Dictionary: On Historical Principles*. Oxford: Oxford University Press (first published 1933).

Ornstein, R.E. (1972) *The Psychology of Consciousness*. San Francisco: W.H. Freeman.

Ovsiankina, M. (1928) 'Die Wiederaufnahme von Interbrochenen Handlungen', *Psychologische Forschung*, 2: 302–89.

Passons, W.R. (1975) *Gestalt Approaches in Counselling*. New York: Holt, Rinehart and Winston.

Pavlov, I.P. (1928) *Lectures on Conditioned Reflexes* (trans. by W.H. Ganff). New York: International Publishers.

Perls, F.S. (1969a) *Ego, Hunger and Aggression*. New York: Vintage Books (first published 1947).

Perls, F.S. (1969b) *Gestalt Therapy Verbatim*. Moab, UT: Real People Press.

Perls, F.F. (1975) 'Group vs. Individual Therapy', pp. 9–15 in J.O. Stevens (ed.), *Gestalt Is*. Moab, UT: Real People Press.

Perls, F.S. (1976) *The Gestalt Approach & Eye Witness to Therapy*. New York: Bantam Books (first published 1973).

Perls, F.S. (1979) 'Planned Psychotherapy', *Gestalt Journal*, 2(2): 5–23.

Perls, F.S., Hefferline, R.F. and Goodman, P. (1951/1969) *Gestalt Therapy: Excitement and Growth in the Human Personality*. New York: Julian Press.

Perls, L. (1977) 'Comments on the New Directions', pp. 221–6 in E.W. Smith (ed.), *The Growing Edge of Gestalt Therapy*. Secaucus, NJ: Citadel Press.

Polster, E. (1985) 'Imprisoned in the Present', *Gestalt Journal*, 8(1): 5–22.

Polster, E. (1987) *Every Person's Life Is Worth a Novel*. New York: W.W. Norton.

Polster, E. and M. Polster (1973) *Gestalt Therapy Integrated: Contours of Theory and Practice*. New York: Random House.

Polster, E. and M. Polster (1974) *Gestalt Therapy Integrated*. New York: Vintage Books (first published 1973).

Polster, E. and M. Polster (1977) 'Gestalt Therapy', pp. 213–16 in B.B. Wolman (ed.), *International Encyclopedia of Neurology, Psychiatry, Psychoanalysis and Psychology* (Vols 1–12). New York: Aesculapius.

Reich, W. (1972) *Character Analysis* (third edition). New York: Simon and Schuster (first published 1945).

Reps, P. (1971) *Zen Flesh, Zen Bones*. Harmondsworth: Penguin Books (first published 1957).

Resnick, R.W. (1984) 'Gestalt Therapy East and West: Bi-Coastal Dialogue, Debate or Debacle?', *Gestalt Journal*, 7(1): 13–32.

Resnick, R.W. (1987) *Personal Communication*.

Rosenblatt, D. (1995) 'In Opposition to "Neo-Gestalt" – Critical Reflections on Present Day Trends in Gestalt Therapy', *British Gestalt Journal*, 4(1): 47–9.

Rosenfeld, E. (1982) 'An Oral History of Gestalt Therapy. Part One: A Conversation with Laura Perls', pp. 3–25 in J. Wysong and E. Rosenfeld (eds), *An Oral History of Gestalt Therapy*. New York: Gestalt Journal.

Rosenthal, R. and L. Jacobson (1968) *Pygmalion in the Classroom: Teacher Expectation and Pupil's Intellectual Development*. New York: Holt, Rinehart and Winston.

Rycroft, C. (1972/1979) *A Critical Dictionary of Psychoanalysis*. Harmondsworth: Penguin Books (first published 1968).

Sartre, J.-P. (1948) *Existentialism and Humanism* (trans. by Philip Mairet). London: Methuen (first published in French 1946).

Sartre, J.-P. (1956) *Being and Nothingness* (trans. by Hazel E. Barnes). New York: Philosophical Library (first published in French 1946).

Simkin, J.S. (1976) *Gestalt Therapy: Mini-Lectures*. Millbrae, CA: Celestial Arts.

Simkin, J.S. and G.M. Yontef (1984) 'Gestalt Therapy', pp. 279–319 in R.J. Corsini (ed.), *Current Psychotherapies*, Itasca, IL: F.E. Peacock.

Smith, E.W. (ed.) (1977) *The Growing Edge of Gestalt Therapy*. Secaucus, NJ: Citadel Press.

Smuts, J. (1926) *Holism and Evolution*. New York: Macmillan.

Smuts, J.C. (1987) *Holism and Evolution*. Cape Town: N & S Press (first published 1926).

Stevens, B. (1970) *Don't Push the River*. Lafayette, CA: Real People Press.

Stevens, B. (1975) 'Body Work', pp. 157–84 in J.O. Stevens (ed.), *Gestalt Is*. Moab, UT: Real People Press.

Stevens, J.O. (ed.) (1975) *Gestalt Is*. Moab, UT: Real People Press.

Stoppard, T. (1993) *Arcadia*. London: Faber and Faber.

Stratford, C.D. and L.W. Brallier (1979) 'Gestalt Therapy with Profoundly Disturbed Persons', *Gestalt Journal*, 2(1): 90–103.

Suzuki, D.T. (1949) *Introduction to Zen Buddhism*. London: John Murray.

Suzuki, D.T. (1972/1974) *Living by Zen*. London: Rider (first published 1950).

Tobin, S.A. (1975) 'Saying Goodbye', pp. 117–28 in J.O. Stevens (ed.), *Gestalt Is*. Moab, UT: Real People Press.

Tobin, S.A. (1983) 'Gestalt Therapy and the Self: Reply to Yontef', *Gestalt Journal*, 6(1): 71–90.

Van De Riet, V., M.P. Korb and J.J. Gorrell (1980/1985) *Gestalt Therapy, An Introduction*. New York: Pergamon Press.

Van Dusen, W. (1975a) 'The Phenomenology of a Schizophrenic Existence', pp. 95–115 in J.O. Stevens (ed.), *Gestalt Is*. Moab, UT: Real People Press.

Van Dusen, W. (1975b) 'Wu Wei, No-mind, and the Fertile Void', pp. 87–93 in J.O. Stevens (ed.), *Gestalt Is*. Moab, UT: Real People Press.

Von Franz, M.-L. (1978) *Time: Rhythm and Repose*. London: Thames and Hudson.

Watts, A.W. (1962/1974) *The Way of Zen*. Harmondsworth: Penguin Books (first published 1957).

Wertheimer, M. (1944) 'Gestalt Theory', *Social Research*, 11(1): 78–99.

Whitmont, E.C. and Y. Kaufmann (1977) 'Analytical Psychology and Gestalt Therapy', pp. 87–102 in E.W. Smith (ed.), *The Growing Edge of Gestalt Therapy*. Secaucus, NJ: Citadel Press.

Whyte, L.L. (1954) *Accent on Form*. New York: Harper.

Wittgenstein, L. (1981/1986) *Tractatus Logico-Philosophicus* (trans. from the German by C.K. Ogden). London: Routledge and Kegan Paul (first published 1922).

Yontef, G.M. (1979a) 'A Review of the Practice of Gestalt Therapy' in F.D. Stephenson (ed.), *Gestalt Therapy Primer*. Springfield, IL: C. Thomas.

Yontef, G.M. (1979b) 'Gestalt Therapy: Clinical Phenomenology', *Gestalt Journal*, 2(1): 27–45.

Yontef, G.M. (1981) 'Gestalt Therapy: A Dialogic Method'. Unpublished manuscript.

Yontef, G.M. (1984) 'Modes of Thinking in Gestalt Therapy', *Gestalt Journal*, 7(1): 33–74.

Yontef, G.M. (1987) 'Gestalt Therapy 1986: A Polemic', *Gestalt Journal*, 10(1): 41–68.

Yontef, G.M. (1988) 'Assimilating Diagnostic and Psychoanalytic Perspectives into Gestalt Therapy', *Gestalt Journal*, 11(1): 5–32.

Yontef, G.M. (1998) 'Dialogic Gestalt Therapy', pp. 82–102 in L.S. Greenberg, G. Lietaer and J.C. Watson (eds), *Handbook of Experiential Psychotherapy*. New York: Guilford Press.

Zeigarnik, B. (1927) Uber das Behalten von Erledigten und Unerledigten Handlungen. *Psychologische Forschung*, 9: 1–85.

Zinker, J. (1978) *Creative Process in Gestalt Therapy*. New York: Vintage Books (first published 1977).

Zinker, J. (1987) 'Gestalt Values: Maturing of Gestalt Therapy', *Gestalt Journal*, 10(1): 69–89.

Index

Compiled by INDEXING SPECIALISTS, 202 Church Road, Hove, East Sussex BN3 2DJ.
Tel: 01273 738299. E-mail: richardr@indexing.co.uk Website: www.indexing.co.uk